DURING SCHOOL HOURS

~~before~~ *after*

DURING SCHOOL HOURS

WHY and **HOW** LifeWise Academy is reinstalling religious education into the *public school day.*

LIFEWISE PRESS

DURING SCHOOL HOURS

By Joel Penton
© 2023 Joel Penton

All rights reserved. No part of this publication may be reproduced or transmitted in any form or by any means, electronic or mechanical, including photocopy, recording or any information storage and retrieval system now known or to be invented, without the permission in writing from the author, except by a reviewer who wishes to quote brief passages in connection with a review written for inclusion in a magazine, newspaper or broadcast.

Published by LifeWise Press
Printed by Lightning Source
Edited by Shannah Hogue
Cover Design by Nathan Lundquist
Page Design & Layout by Jon Ringger
Penton, Joel, 2023
[DURING SCHOOL HOURS]
Education-Religious Education-Education
ISBN 979-8-9876175-1-9
Manufactured in the United States of America

DEDICATION

For the thousands of men and women in the LifeWise family who are making sacrifices every day to impact future generations.

CONTENTS

LifeWise Story: My Story—The Day That Changed Everything 8

An Important Clarification: What This Book Is and Isn't About 12

PART 1
Why WE'RE REINSTALLING RELIGIOUS EDUCATION

Chapter 1: Undoing Public Education
WHY Religious Education Was Removed 24

Chapter 2: Unintended Consequences
WHY Removing Religious Education Costs Everything 38

Chapter 3: Unexpected Impact
WHY Reinstalling Religious Education Is a Game Changer 54

Chapter 4: An Obvious Choice
WHY Religious Education Creates True Neutrality 76

PART 2
How WE'RE REINSTALLING RELIGIOUS EDUCATION WITH LIFEWISE ACADEMY

Chapter 5: A New Fit That's Kind of Old
    HOW Religious Education Integrates Legally 96

Chapter 6: 70 Years in the Wilderness
    HOW Released Time Has Survived 112

Chapter 7: Crafting the Right Tool (Part 1)
    HOW LifeWise Academy Was Born 136

Chapter 8: Crafting the Right Tool (Part 2)
    HOW LifeWise Academy Started to Blow Up (in a Good Way) 158

Chapter 9: Time for a Movement?
    HOW LifeWise Looks Today 182

Chapter 10: The Last Missing Piece
    HOW You Fit In 198

EXTRA *things*

Appendix 1: Nitty Gritty LifeWise FAQs 211

Appendix 2: Even More Impact 219

Acknowledgements 230

Endnotes 233

Bibliography 243

MY STORY

Scan to Watch Video

A LIFEWISE STORY

"My Story: The Day That Changed Everything"

I grew up in Van Wert, Ohio, a small town in the northwest corner of the state. After high school, I attended The Ohio State University where I played football on the Buckeyes' defensive line (Go Bucks!). I wasn't a marquee player, but I did earn some varsity letters, and they gave me a 2002 National Championship ring so I can prove that I was on the team.

After I graduated, I became a motivational speaker in middle schools and high schools all over the country, engaging with teachers and administrators and challenging students to live a life of commitment. I also spoke at faith-based outreach events after school hours where students could come back and hear about what really gives my life purpose. Along the way I founded a nonprofit speakers' bureau that has now, by God's grace, touched more than three thousand schools and two million students nationwide. It's been a fun ride.

But I never lost my ties to Van Wert. So when a local released time program called Cross Over the Hill dedicated their newly built Bible education facility, they invited me to speak at the ceremony (probably because my sister was on the board). And I gladly agreed (also probably because my sister was on the board). But I was completely unprepared for just how much my life was about to change.

As I prepared for the speech, I learned more about the incredible program, and my mind was absolutely blown. "Wait, they're teaching the Bible to public school students DURING SCHOOL HOURS? How is this possible? And 95% of the entire elementary school is enrolled? What??"

After the ceremony, I sat in on their board meeting, and they asked me to help them answer one question: Why don't more communities have programs like this?

Sitting in that meeting, a new vision for what was possible popped fully formed into my head. On the drive home that evening, I had a clear-as-day picture in my mind of all that could be accomplished if we could spread what this one program had done.

- ✦ In Van Wert, nearly every student in the school was enrolled in the program and loved it. What if other students could have a similar, positive experience?

- ✦ Teachers and administrators talked about the positive effects the program had. What if other schools could experience the same positive influence?

- ✦ The whole community—parents, churches, local leaders—was supporting the school in effective and truly helpful ways. What if other schools received similar support? What if community members were just waiting and hoping for an opportunity to get involved?

- ✦ And most of all, what if we could bring all of it together in a usable, effective, replicable model?

My vision was clear but uncertain. There was a lot to consider and research. But if we could do it, I was convinced that we could change the very face of public education.

Over five years later, I am even more convinced.

So I wrote a book.

AN IMPORTANT CLARIFICATION

What This Book Is and Isn't About

I've written this book to share two things with you:

1. Why religious education should be reinstalled into the public school day.

2. How any community can do it successfully and immediately.

So why am I qualified to discuss these things? Simple—because we're doing it.

I'm the founder and CEO of LifeWise Academy, a nonprofit ministry that provides religious education for public school students during school hours. And we—my team and I, along with dozens of local communities—are making it happen *right now*.

The concept is simple. We transport students from their school to a nearby location, provide a weekly Bible education class, and return them to their schools.

And did I mention that it all takes place *during school hours*?

Those three little words are what make LifeWise Academy a ground-breaking opportunity.

When people first hear about LifeWise, they usually think it sounds made up or illegal. But it's not.

It's a little-known approach called released time religious instruction. And it's a game-changer. In fact, we are convinced that released time has been the single greatest missed opportunity to impact the next generation of public school students.

For decades, ministries have been impacting public school students *before* and *after* school. But the students who most need to be reached are often missed due to logistical and scheduling challenges. What we're doing is different—because it's *during* school hours, we're able to better integrate into the school's culture and reach the previously unreachable.

When people first hear about LifeWise, they usually think it sounds made up or illegal. But it's not.

Our program is entirely real and fully legal since the Supreme Court ruled on this decades ago. But the concept has been just sitting there, somewhat dormant. Until now.

Right now, we are taking big steps to provide the opportunity of released time to districts everywhere. And things are starting to move. In fact, they're starting to *explode*.

LifeWise Academy is only a few years old, but its reach is growing literally by the day. At the time of this writing, we are serving more than one hundred schools nationwide, and we're actively engaged with several hundred more communities who are taking steps toward starting a program for their local public school students.

What we are seeing and experiencing is bigger than we ever imagined. It's starting to feel like a movement. Like a revolution. And we are excited—hard-to-sleep excited—about the program and its possibilities.

Which is why I wrote this book. In these chapters, I'll be sharing all about the exciting opportunity that is released time and LifeWise Academy.

But before we dive into what this book is about—the WHY and the HOW of reinstalling religious education into the public school day—let's get clear about what it *isn't* about.

WHAT I'M LEAVING OUT

This book is not about *politics*.

For most people, their views on public education are directly connected to their political views. But none of those views are the point of this book. I won't be addressing right-wing or left-wing ideas or political parties or anyone's favorite candidates. There is room in this book for people of all political persuasions, and no one has to think (or vote) like me in order to consider or appreciate what we'll discuss in these pages.

This book is not about *the merits of public education*.

I will not be discussing the value of public education itself or whether students should attend public schools. Our approach assumes that public schools are a permanent part of our education landscape. There are many who are fully committed to public education and those who recommend other tracks (like private schools, charter schools, or homeschool), and there is much we could say about each option. This book is simply not the place for that debate.

The one thing I will say on this topic—because it is important—is that I believe all educators are heroes. They serve their students and communities in selfless, sacrificial ways. They give their time, money, and hearts to seeing their students thrive. And they are to be supported and commended.

This book is not about *the methods of public education*.

I will not be exploring the systems and models, past or present, of public education. I will mention them because it's necessary to make my point. But this book will not be debating how *this model* is so much better than *that model* or which model I like best. Because the issue isn't the model at all. No matter what model schools choose, my argument will remain the same: it is imperative that we once again include religious education during school hours.

This book is not about *the good old days.*

There were many good things that we can point to about education in the past, as well as things we wouldn't want to repeat. Really, there's no such thing as "the good old days," so this book isn't a call to turn back the clock in any way. Instead, this book is about the future. I'm going to lay out strategies—practical, positive, real-world strategies—that will work in today's society with its new and unique needs and in the decades to come.

Lastly, this book is not about *theology.*

Full disclosure: LifeWise Academy is a Christian religious education program that teaches the Bible. But this book is not my attempt to convince you about my theological views. There are great books for that, which I'm happy to recommend, but my theological position is not the point. Regardless of my theology, or yours, it's easy to see the benefits that religious education can bring to the public school system and its students. But let me repeat: specific points of theology will not appear anywhere in these pages. (You're welcome.)

THE TWO-PART ROADMAP

As I said before, this book is about the WHY and HOW of reinstalling religious education into the public school day.

But that vision could be more clear. So here's the detailed summary of my goal for this book:

"In this book, I'm going to show you WHY reinstalling religious education into the public school day is our best opportunity to positively impact students, schools and communities and lay out a clear plan for HOW to do it legally and effectively." (Joel)

Let me break down the highlights.

"I'm going to show you"

Everything you're about to read is factually, provably true. I can back up my claims with both real-world examples and well-crafted academic studies. I'm not trying to hoodwink you. This is not a bait-and-switch. Over the next ten chapters, I'm going to demonstrate, clearly and effectively, that what I'm proposing can and does work.

"our best opportunity"

Reinstalling religious education isn't the only option we have to help students and schools. But I believe it is the greatest missed opportunity in education right now. It is powerful, positive, and extremely underused. What lies before us is a clear and effective path we would be entirely remiss to ignore.

"to positively impact students, schools and communities"

We all want to see our students succeed academically and develop into fully mature, thriving humans. We want to see schools supported and better equipped to fulfill their mission. And we want to see communities and families come alongside both students and schools in powerful and positive ways.

I have seen all of this happen in real schools, in real communities, with real students. This isn't wishful thinking. It's hope. Hope that comes when religious education is reinstalled into public education.

"a clear plan for how to do it legally and effectively"

The path forward is released time religious instruction. The tool we've created to forge that path is LifeWise Academy. It is legal and effective, and I will show you exactly how we can make it work. The bulk of the book will lay out this plan in detail and address objections.

Objections like these:

- ✦ What about separation of church and state? (check out chapter 5)
- ✦ But religious instruction isn't the purpose of public education, Joel! (see chapter 2)
- ✦ Which religions would be taught? Won't it offend people? (that's chapter 5, too)
- ✦ What makes LifeWise so special? (you want chapters 7 and 8)
- ✦ So how do you fit LifeWise classes into the schedule anyway? (check out the FAQ appendix)

I hear these questions all the time. Because the issues we're wrestling with are not new. Neither is the debate. And interestingly, neither is the solution.

But I'm proposing a new look at an old approach. One that really works. One that could change everything. And one that begins by understanding WHY we need to reinstall religious education in the first place.

Three Ways
TO READ THIS BOOK

#1 "I'm not sure whether religious education for public school students is a good idea."

#2 "I already know religious education is a good idea. I want to know how to get it done."

#3 "I don't have a great attention span. I just like stories."

READ STRAIGHT THROUGH, BEGINNING TO END.

SKIP TO PART TWO FOR THE GOODS...
and come back to read Part One afterward so you can engage with others.

READ ALL RED PAGES SCATTERED THROUGHOUT.
Those are super quick stories and tidbits. Also read chapters 7 and 8 which contain the story of LifeWise. Those chapters even have pictures.

Is something really missing?

PART

ONE

Why

We're Reinstalling Religious Education

CHAPTER 01

UNDOING PUBLIC EDUCATION
WHY Religious Education Was Removed

A lot of people see what we're doing with LifeWise Academy, incorporating religious instruction into the public school day, as "innovative."

It's kind of ironic. Because once upon a time, no one would have considered having public schools without it.

Of course, all that changed years ago. Religious education has long since been removed from public education. And whether or not you celebrate that development, my point is—it happened.

Religious education was at one time part of American education, and now it isn't. It was, at one point, considered central to education's purpose, and now it's been effectively eliminated.

Some readers may call that progress. Others may disagree. But in this chapter, I simply want to lay out a very brief outline of how the removal happened. I'll organize the account into four stages.

STAGE ONE: COLONIES, COMMUNITIES, AND THE CHURCH
Early 1600s to Late 1700s – Religion as the Focus of Education

Education in Colonial America didn't just include religious instruction, it was born out of religious motivations.

Teaching people to read was one of the primary goals of early American education. Each colony established "local varieties of *fee* and *free* schools"[1] because, from the first settlers' arrival, they believed "all children ought to be able to read, no matter how low their station or how poor their circumstances."[2]

And it was religious ideals that drove this desire.

The early colonists wanted their children to be literate primarily so that they could read the Bible. Basic reading texts were almost entirely religious.[3] For example, quotations from the Bible made up almost 90% of early editions of *The New England Primer*, one of the most popular textbooks of the time.[4]

Laws were even passed that emphasized this religious focus. The Old Deluder Satan Act, passed in Massachusetts in 1647, is perhaps the most striking example. It required families and communities to teach children to read, stating explicitly that teaching children to read prevented them from growing up ignorant of the Bible.[5]

And this approach was typical throughout the colonies in every type of school—the Puritan approach of New England, the parochial schools of the middle colonies, or the hired tutors of the South.[6] "Religious instruction was the main purpose of their existence and the principal content of their curriculum."[7]

Of course, public schools as we know them did not exist yet. But it was Christian leaders, including Reverend John Cotton, who established the Boston Latin School (BLS), considered by many to be the first public school in America. Founded in 1635, the BLS was publicly funded from its inception, and its first admission requirements included reading several verses from the Bible.[8]

STAGE TWO: COMMON SCHOOLS WITH COMPROMISE

Early 1800s to Mid 1800s – Religion Integrated with Curriculum

By the early 1800s, there was a growing call for universal education, run by the state and supported by taxes.[9] Over time, more local schools were established that provided education beyond basic literacy to an ever-growing number of students. These "common schools" were the forerunners of public schools as we know them today.

Curriculum in the common schools "maintained a decidedly religious tone,"[10] but as the movement grew, church and denominational distinctions were often removed in favor of general religious or moral principles.

Horace Mann was a key figure in this shift. Called the "father of public education," Mann "advocated instruction in universal Christian principles and values that would allow students to make their own moral judgments."[11]

To many at the time, this compromise seemed the only way forward for an increasingly diverse population. They believed that general religious principles would still provide the moral development that students and society needed. But as time went on, explicitly biblical material was minimized or replaced in the curriculum.

The McGuffey Reader is a helpful illustration.

In the mid-1830s, William Holmes McGuffey compiled the four-volume series called *The McGuffey Readers*. These textbooks, especially the first two, became the primary curriculum for common schools for the next sixty years.[12] More than 120 million copies were sold between 1839 and 1920,[13] a rate similar to sales of the Bible and *Webster's Dictionary*.

Religious instruction came to be seen as incompatible with the standardized approach to education.

McGuffey, an experienced teacher, believed "religion and education to be interrelated and essential to a healthy society."[14] So when they were first published, the readers contained clear biblical teachings.

But as society changed, so did the *McGuffey Reader*. By the late 1800s, American society "sought less moral and spiritual content in their schoolbooks."[15] As a result, later editions of the reader, which McGuffey neither wrote nor approved, replaced the biblical lessons with "middle-class civil religion, morality, and values."[16]

STAGE THREE: COMPULSORY AND (IN)COMPATIBLE

Mid 1800s to Early 1900s – Religious Content Separated and Set Aside

Between 1850 and 1920, an incredibly short time for such a major shift, public education became the norm across the country. It was paid for by tax money and organized by state-level Boards of Education.[17] And by 1918, every state had passed compulsory attendance laws, requiring every child to be part of these new public schools.[18]

The school system itself was an entirely "new social institution" intended to address not only education reform, but also industrialization, immigration, and new social issues.[19] In the process, however, it also created a rift between religious and public education.

Religious instruction came to be seen as incompatible with the standardized approach to education. Significant developments in academia and culture also accelerated the removal of religion from schools.

Let me give you a couple of examples.

A LIFEWISE
"Tidbit"

Madalyn Murray O'Hair, the atheist who famously fought for the removal of prayer from public schools, studied at Ashland University in Ashland, Ohio. My friend, Pastor John Bouquet, leads a church and the local ministerial association in the Ashland area. On several occasions I've heard Pastor John mention O'Hair. In light of her legacy in Ashland, Pastor John says that he feels a particular responsibility to create religious education opportunities for Ashland area students. Due in large part to his efforts, LifeWise now provides Bible education for students in several school districts in Ashland County—including Ashland City Schools (where Ms. O'Hair attended college) as well as the Hillsdale district (where Ms. O'Hair resided).

1: The Rise of Science

Darwin's *On the Origins of the Species* was published in 1859. The book cast serious doubt on religious answers to questions about humanity, its origins and its importance as a species.[20]

Darwin's theory "eliminated the need for a supernatural Creator" and claimed that "naturalistic processes" were sufficient to explain our world.[21] And while he himself never broke officially with the church, Darwin's ideas grew in influence until most people assumed that evolutionary theory had replaced biblical or religious beliefs about the world, its origins and its meaning.

Science was seen to hold all the answers. And if that was the case, as Darwin seemed to have proved, then there was little need to discuss the Bible or its teachings in school. It was simply irrelevant.

2: The Rise of Secularism

If science freed humanity from the relevance of religious thought, secularism actively removed it from the public sphere, including public education.

John Dewey, one of the most influential thinkers of the early 1900s, is the best example.

His goal for education was philosophical, psychological, and practical. But it left almost no space for anything religious.[22] In 1899, he wrote *The School and Society*, "a 'scientific' appraisal of public education in which religion had almost no role."[23]

As one writer put it, "Dewey wished for supernatural belief to be swept into the dustbin of history by the broom of the scientific method and saw himself as the one doing the sweeping."[24]

In the early decades of the twentieth century, Dewey's views spread and changed how and what schools taught. By the 1930s, the Bible had almost disappeared from the curriculum of public schools. A degree of religious influence, practice and teachings remained, but they were relegated mostly to holidays or special events.[25] And as culture became still more secular after 1930, even those vestiges began to be uninstalled from public schools.

STAGE FOUR: THE COURTS

Mid 1900s to Present – Religion Expelled from Schools

During the 1940s and 1950s, the issue of religion and public education moved into the courts. The Supreme Court's decisions during those twenty years effectively finished the process of removing religion and religious education from the public schools. Three specific cases will illustrate the point.

Everson v. Board of Education (1947)

A New Jersey taxpayer challenged the use of school buses to take children to private and religious schools. While the practice was allowed to continue, the decision stated that Thomas Jefferson's wall of separation must be kept "high and impregnable" to keep the state neutral, igniting an ongoing conversation about what it means to "establish religion."[26]

Engel v. Vitale (1962)

A New York school district adopted a nondenominational prayer that students voluntarily recited every morning. Several families sued the district, saying the prayer violated the First Amendment, and won. One of the most famous First Amendment cases, it has been the basis for declaring prayer in school unconstitutional in later cases.[27]

Abington School District v. Schempp (1963)

In this case, Bible verses including the Lord's Prayer were read in a Pennsylvania district without comment. A local family sued, again claiming this was a violation of the First Amendment. Along with *Murray v. Curlett (1963)*, this decision forbid the reading of Bible verses in schools, though the academic study of the Bible was allowed.[28]

Over the course of twenty years, these Supreme Court cases, and others, codified the expulsion of religious education from American public schools. Religion was officially kicked out of class.

THE REMOVAL OF RELIGIOUS EDUCATION

At one time, religious education and public education in America were indistinguishable. The former helped create the latter. But over time, they differentiated and separated. Religious education was uninstalled from public schools.

Of course I realize it isn't enough to simply point out that we removed religious education. If something is harmful or not useful, removing it isn't a problem. We don't regret pulling weeds from our garden, but pulling a vegetable plant is a problem. One we celebrate. The other we mourn.

So we can't just ask *whether* religious education was removed. It clearly was. Now we have to ask, "Was removing religious education beneficial, or did its removal hurt public education?"

The answer to that question is the subject of our next chapter.

TIM'S STORY

Scan to Watch Video

A LIFEWISE STORY

"Tim and His Grandmother"

Tim's story begins at his Grandma Stoller's house during a family get-together when he was young.

The family had gathered on a Sunday afternoon like they so often did, but on this particular week, his grandmother was very upset. She was an elementary school teacher at the local school, Payne Elementary, and that week, she'd received some frustrating news.

She had, for years, led a short Bible lesson with her students at the beginning of each school day, and someone had, apparently, complained. As a result, the administrators of her school told her she could no longer teach a Bible lesson to her class.

As she told the family all about it, everyone could see that she was angry and sad. She was disappointed. And she had no choice but to stop teaching a Bible lesson.

Tim is helping communities do for their local schools what his grandmother was told she could not do.

At the time, Tim was only a child, but it left him with a vivid memory and lesson—*you can't share your faith during school.*

Fast forward a few dozen years.

When Tim first heard about the possibility of a released time program in Van Wert, one of his initial hesitations was that he didn't think teaching the Bible during school hours was allowed. After all, his grandmother had been told to stop.

But as Tim learned more about the proposed initiative, he realized it was both possible and legal. Tim became a founding board member of Cross Over the Hill, the Van Wert released time program. Currently Tim serves on the national board of LifeWise Academy.

Tim is helping communities do for their local schools what his grandmother was told she could not do. And as of 2020, Payne Elementary, the same school where Tim's grandmother taught all those years ago, is served by LifeWise Academy.

So now, decades after Tim's grandmother was told not to, *more than 70% of the students of Payne Elementary hear a fully legal Bible lesson during their school day.*

✦ ✦ ✦

CHAPTER 02

UNINTENDED CONSEQUENCES
WHY Removing Religious Education Costs Everything

We have removed religious education from public education in America.

There's no question about that. But there is a question of whether or not separating the two was harmful.

If removing religious education has cost us nothing, then there isn't much need for programs like LifeWise Academy. But if public education was harmed by its removal, then we have real motivation to reinstall it. So how can we tell?

When you remove a block from a Jenga tower, it's immediately apparent whether removing that particular piece was a good choice. If the block was necessary, the tower falls. Game over.

But unlike board games, most real-world outcomes aren't so immediate. It's not until much later that we find how much we actually needed the thing we left out.

Like with oil in a car.

Many people don't change the oil in their

cars every three thousand miles, as is recommended. And what happens? Nothing terrible, at least not right away. And thanks to warning lights, most people will get the oil changed often enough to prevent any issues.

But there are always a few people who don't.

Nothing bad happened when they missed one oil change, so they let it go longer. They brush it off. They forget about it. Until one day, they've gone so long and the oil is so low that the engine seizes up and the car stops.

In case you didn't know, this is very bad (and very expensive to fix).

Like with oil in our cars, negative consequences aren't always obvious at first. But if we remove something important, like oil, there will eventually be problems we can see.

HEEDING THE WARNING LIGHTS

After nearly a hundred years, there's plenty of evidence to indicate that something has gone wrong with public education. Like warning lights on the dashboard, the problems are, unfortunately, easy to see.

In fact, it would be easy to write a whole chapter filled with loads of statistics and stories about the "failing" public school system.

It could start with the drop in literacy we cannot seem to overcome.[1] I could quote concerns about reading proficiency,[2] falling test scores,[3] and how far behind the world we are in math[4] and science.[5] We could discuss the achievement gap[6] and lack of educational success in at-risk buildings and school districts.[7]

And those are only the academic issues.

When we include the realities of school environments, the picture becomes even bleaker. The rise in truancy[8] and violent behavior.[9] The rising rates of risk behaviors.[10] Rampant bullying.[11] The entirely new concerns caused by social media and our digital age.[12]

And I could finish with the reality that it is more normal for our students to be unhealthy mentally and emotionally than to be healthy.[13] Despite years of social-emotional learning, the rates of anxiety and depression are skyrocketing.[14] Suicide numbers are rising every year.[15]

Thankfully, I'm not going to write that chapter.

First, you already know most of those things. Second, there are lots of books and articles out there you can read on those topics. And most importantly, telling horror stories and reciting negative statistics won't help anything.

I'm simply pointing out that all of those problems are on full display, they are the talking points of countless meetings across education, and everyone agrees that each of the problems must be addressed.

And they should. In fact, we will look at how religious education affects each of those specific areas in the next chapter.

But right now, I want to invite you to consider that the visible issues we face in education are actually symptoms of a deeper, more fundamental issue. When we uninstalled religious instruction from public education, we pulled the wrong Jenga block. We tampered with the foundation on which the whole structure rests.

What I mean is that the visible problems are, at least in part, the outworking of a failure to fully pursue the true purpose of education.

THE PURPOSE PROBLEM

So what's the purpose of education? I think it's something most of us can actually agree on: **to produce well-rounded humans, equipped to thrive individually and as members of society.**

I've spoken in a thousand schools over the last fifteen years, and every one of them wants to produce well-rounded students, equipped to thrive. In fact, that's one of the key reasons speakers like me are invited to speak.

We simply cannot produce well-rounded students without religious instruction.

This purpose is reflected in our educational models. The most popular one right now is the Whole Child model. Launched by ASCD, an educational nonprofit, and currently in use in over 1,500 schools, the Whole Child approach seeks to establish "student conditions leading to success in life and learning."[16]

And so our public schools provide a great variety of disciplines and opportunities. We have gym class, health class, financial literacy and social-emotional learning. We give recess and extra time on tests and serve breakfast and lunch every day. There is art and music, along with the foundations of reading, language arts, math and science.

But there's a problem. Despite the popularity and vocabulary of the Whole Child model, we are not, in fact, teaching the whole child. We've left a gaping hole. There are no moral-spiritual lessons. There's no religious instruction.

The only thing we say about the moral-spiritual aspect in school is that we aren't supposed to talk about the moral-spiritual side of things in school.

And that's not educating the *whole* child.

We simply cannot produce well-rounded students without religious instruction. Because the moral and spiritual part of our humanity isn't just one equal piece of the whole. It is actually the *key piece* to the whole.

A car doesn't need leather seats, but it does need an engine. Chocolate chip cookies can have a variety of chocolate chips, but they won't rise without baking soda.

With anything, some pieces are flexible. But some, like engines and baking soda, are essential. If you don't have those vital ones, you won't get the outcome you want. And that's exactly what's going on in public education.[17]

That's because it is in religious and spiritual education that we engage with many essentials for a thriving life. Here are two examples.

ESSENTIAL #1: WORLDVIEW—UNDERSTANDING THE WHOLE

Worldview is the big category for how we interpret and understand all of reality as a whole. If you think that sounds a lot like religion, you're right. Someone smarter than me explains the close relationship between religion and worldview in this way:

> *Religion* and *worldview* are similar terms. Usually people use the word *religion* to refer to religious practices such as a form of worship or moral guidelines. *Worldview* usually describes how that religion's ideas about where everything came from (cause), what is real (nature), and how we ought to live (purpose) come together to form a vision for society.[18]

Simple knowledge and facts of our natural world only get at the "what" of things. But worldview questions of **cause**, **nature** and **purpose** get at the "why." These are the deepest, most fundamental questions of life, and they must not be ignored if we want to produce well-rounded students, equipped to thrive.

A robust worldview doesn't only speak to the deeper questions of life, it also determines how we make sense and use of everything else, including the various academic disciplines.

Think of it like a wheel. Every wheel has three parts: rim, spokes, and hub. (I'm imagining a bike tire or the wheel of a covered wagon. Got the picture? Good.)

The outer rim is the whole-person outcome we want education to develop. It's that meaningful, well-rounded life that can take our students anywhere they want to go.

The spokes support the outer rim, filling out the shape so the wheel can roll. In education, the spokes are the classes, activities, knowledge and tools that schools provide. Our students need those things. Without them, the outer rim (the thriving life) will collapse.

A LIFEWISE

"Tidbit"

I have a Muslim friend named Omar. Omar is an attorney and sits on the city council where I live. Omar is also a big proponent of LifeWise. Why does a Muslim support a Christian program? Well, maybe it's partly because we're friends. But that's not what Omar says. Omar says that kids need roots to anchor their lives. He wants to see LifeWise succeed because he believes it will help give students roots to grow a stable foundation on which they can thrive in life.

Religious instruction is essential to the development of wisdom.

But the spokes won't work without a center anchor to tie them all together.[19] That is the hub. And a person's worldview functions as a hub. It's where all the knowledge, skills and disciplines fit together so the wheel works as a unified whole.

Everyone has a worldview. We all have to make sense of the deeper questions of life and how everything fits together. And it's only through religious instruction that students can fully engage with these issues to build a well-rounded, thriving life.

ESSENTIAL #2: WISDOM—UNDERSTANDING MORAL CHOICE

Religious instruction is essential to the development of wisdom. No amount of factual knowledge or scientific inquiry can guide our students in the lifelong need to be able to make wise moral judgements and then act on them.

C.S. Lewis compares the need for morality to sheet music. Our well-informed morality directs when to exercise our various natural instincts and impulses like the sheet music directs musicians. He wrote:

> Think once again of a piano. It has not got two kinds of notes on it, the "right" notes and the "wrong" ones. Every single note is right at one time and wrong at another. The Moral Law ... is something which makes a kind of tune (the tune we call goodness or right conduct) by directing the instincts.[20]

According to Lewis, the moral aspect of our humanness enables us to thrive the way sheet music enables a pianist or an orchestra to perform. All our instincts, talents and skills are like the notes we play, but when and how to engage those notes are at the heart of wisdom.

Just knowing the notes is never enough. People in the twentieth century were more educated than any previous century, and yet it was the bloodiest by far. We weren't made more moral with all that knowledge; we just got smarter about how to kill each other.

Knowledge, by itself, isn't good or bad. But it can be used to accomplish either. In the original *Jurassic Park* movie, Jeff Goldblum's character, Malcolm, says to Hammond, the park's creator, "Your scientists were so preoccupied with whether they could, they didn't stop to think if they should."[21]

And while I know quoting a movie from 1993 totally dates me, the quote is still true. *Can* and *should* are not the same thing. And it is wisdom that helps us tell the difference.

Through their education, students will develop their capacity for what they *can do* in life. They need moral-spiritual instruction to help them understand what they *should do*.

All the classes and knowledge and tools we are handing our students are good. But they aren't wisdom. Our students need the wisdom that comes from religious education. No other subject matter is able to provide the moral framework that students will need in order to make choices in this world.

RESTORING THE MISSING PIECE

Removing religious education from public education eliminated a key piece of our humanity from the schools. And now we're attempting to produce well-rounded, thriving students with one arm tied behind our backs. By reinstalling religious education, we can begin once again to empower our students to develop the spiritual capacity to understand the world more fully and choose more wisely.

Which brings us back to all the doom-and-gloom statistics I didn't share at the beginning of this chapter. Because, if I were reading this book, I'd be wondering just how I know that literacy rates, mental health and other practical issues have been affected by removing religious education.

First, that's a very legitimate question. And second, it has a simple answer.

We know it's true because when we put the spiritual back into education, all of those issues—every single one of them—improves.

Which is what our next chapter is all about. I'm about to show you the provable, positive impact religious education has on our students and schools.

VINCE'S'S STORY

Scan to
Watch Video

A LIFEWISE STORY

"Vince's Story"

Vince Coleman grew up in the inner city on the east side of Columbus, Ohio. His neighborhood, Greenbrier, was so rough that many referred to it as "Uzi Alley."

Vince didn't have much connection to church growing up. He doesn't remember any ministry or church reaching out or influencing him as a kid except one. One church from the suburbs brought a bus in on Sunday mornings to take kids to their church.

Vince says, "They didn't know what they were getting themselves into—and neither did we."

When he attended, he didn't behave well, and he was not invited back. But he does remember hearing John 3:16 for the first time there, and he believes that planted seed made a difference in his life.

Vince grew up, graduated from Columbus City Schools, and served in the military. And eventually, Vince came to faith. He also began a career in education.

For a few years, Vince served as a middle school principal for Columbus City Schools. But as he grew in his faith,

Now under Vince's leadership, LifeWise is serving over twenty schools in Central Ohio.

became an elder in his church, and interacted with families at school, he became convinced that the biggest issues facing kids aren't math and reading—the biggest issues are at home.

So Vince left the education world to join a nonprofit that helps meet the practical needs of families in the inner city. But even that wasn't enough. As he learned more, he concluded that the issues at home are the result of something even deeper. They are issues of the heart.

Vince began to consider how he could use his experiences to impact his community on a spiritual level.

Around that same time, Vince was first introduced to LifeWise Academy. His jaw dropped when he heard that students could attend Bible classes during school hours. Not only that, but LifeWise was looking for someone to lead the charge in Central Ohio, particularly in inner-city Columbus.

Vince's entire life seemed to have been leading to that moment, and he dove in enthusiastically. Now, under Vince's leadership, LifeWise is serving over twenty schools in Central Ohio. Instead of busing kids out of the community on Sundays, Vince is using LifeWise Academy to bring the Bible directly to public school students during their school day.

✦ ✦ ✦

CHAPTER 03

UNEXPECTED IMPACT
WHY Reinstalling Religious Education Is a Game Changer

Not long ago, I had breakfast with a local superintendent.

He had a reputation for being opposed to religious programs in his district, so I was intrigued by his request. I had no idea what he wanted to discuss.

At breakfast, we chatted about football, some mutual friends and OSU (Go Bucks!), and then he shifted abruptly to his point.

"Joel, what is your vision for LifeWise Academy in my district?"

I took a moment to answer. "Well, there is no vision for your district, really. We don't have any hidden agenda. LifeWise Academy is a tool we offer to all communities. If your community wants to use LifeWise, we're ready to help."

His response floored me. "Well, we're ready," he said.

I must have looked stunned because he continued, "Our students need values, Joel. Other administrators I know have nothing but good things to say about LifeWise and its influence in their districts. So just tell me my next steps. I'll do whatever I can to get it running in my district."[1]

THE (NOT SO) HIDDEN TRUTH

I have talked to a lot of administrators, both as a public school speaker and as the founder of LifeWise. While I was not expecting that particular administrator's response, to be honest, I was not surprised at all that this was the feedback he had gotten.

At that point, LifeWise Academy was live in over twenty local school districts, and literally dozens more were in the works. We already knew that our program is effective. Administrators have seen these positive trends in every district that LifeWise serves.

Let me give you just one example. One school district served by LifeWise recently reviewed the data on the students who were most frequently referred to the principal's office for behavioral reasons. The students who did not attend LifeWise had increased numbers of office referrals from the first to second semester while the office referrals for students who did attend LifeWise dropped by more than 60 percent.

But these effects are not new or surprising. The positive impact of religion and religious education has been recognized for decades. And while researchers do not agree on exactly why the positive results exist,[2] they are almost unanimous that religion and religious education have a clear, significant, and positive impact on students.

Let me break that down.

The link is *clear* because it exists even when researchers control for other variables. And it isn't just measurable; it is *significant*. The positive influence of religion on education is highly correlated. And the link is *positive*, meaning that the students and their outcomes are better when religion is included in their education.

Most powerfully, this clear, significant and positive impact appears in exactly the four major areas that administrators, teachers, parents, and community members are already deeply concerned about—character education, mental health, academic outcomes and community involvement.

BEFORE WE START

I should warn you now, though, there is a lot of information in this chapter. And there's so much more that I had to leave out.

Many of these studies are academic in tone. The results are filled with percentages and citations and references to even more studies. And this is the longest chapter in the book.

So you may be seriously tempted to skim, but I encourage you to take the time to let it all sink in.

Because these studies, numbers and research do not lie. Religious education has a *very* powerful and positive impact on students and schools. And seeing it all laid out like this is actually very exciting.

So let's get started with those four areas of impact.

AREA OF IMPACT #1: CHARACTER EDUCATION

As we saw in chapter 2, we want our students to thrive, but to do that, they need to develop good character.

> Character ... provides the foundation for everything else. Without qualities such as good judgment, responsibility, the ability to overcome difficulties, and self-discipline ... students will be handicapped in all areas of their lives. Character underlies personal relationships and personal achievement.[3]

Character is particularly necessary in today's digital society where our kids face opportunities and dangers that have never existed before.[4] In our fast-paced, online world, where both information and decisions are presented to students at top speed, character is what will anchor them and help them cope—wisely and effectively.[5]

A LIFEWISE

"Tidbit"

LifeWise has already seen practical evidence of character change. Not long ago, some students at a school that LifeWise serves got in a bit of trouble during recess. While the teacher was dealing with one of the students who'd been involved, a second young man came back to confess that he, too, had been involved. "We just talked about honesty at LifeWise," he told her, "so I knew I needed to tell the truth about what I'd done."

Unfortunately, many students now have to develop good character, as well as math and reading, at school.

Teachers and administrators have shared this reality with me over and over. "You know Joel, these days it's not enough to simply educate students. You have to be their parent as well," they say. Or, as one principal admitted, "We have a crisis of character."

To deal with this crisis, dozens of character education programs have been created, each one claiming to instill character, promote prosocial behaviors or develop social-emotional maturity in our students.

But religion and religious education have the same (or better) positive impact on character as any of these new programs, even in the twenty-first century. We'll look at three areas where this is true: general character, delinquency and risk behaviors.

General Character

The lack of character often shows up as bullying, a loss of decision-making skills and an inability to connect and engage with others. However, the loss of "respect, trust and responsibility"[6] can be offset by adding religion to the equation.

When the National Council on Crime and Delinquency studied a released time religious instruction program in Oakland, California, they found that studying the Bible along with their school curriculum helped the students develop good character.

According to the report, engaging with Bible lessons and positive adult mentors introduced the students to "themes that support positive character development that can lay a strong foundation for healthy and moral behavior through adolescence and adulthood."[7]

Honesty

Because it is easy to pinpoint, honesty is often the focus of studies on character. And it also demonstrates the positive impact of religion.

In one study, for example, a professor purposely mis-graded a test. After going over the answers, he asked students to let him know if their grades were wrong. Based on an earlier questionnaire, the results were clear: "45 percent of weekly [church] attenders were honest, compared with 13 percent of those who never or rarely attended church."[8]

Delinquency and Violence

Good character also combats the rising rates of truancy and school violence,[9] and once again, religion has a powerful impact.

Rodney Stark, a leading expert on religion and sociology, reports that "religious American teenagers are more likely to attend school regularly (rather than be truants)"[10] and that "religious Americans are far less likely to have dropped out of school."[11]

Like truancy, violence is also reduced by religious engagement because religion tends to "crowd out negative influences"[12] and encourage good behavior, making its influence doubly effective.[13]

According to one study, a survey of 247 studies published over 60 years "reported a positive effect of religion on reducing crime, deviance, and delinquency—often a very strong effect."[14]

Risk Behaviors

For most schools, though, character is most important for discouraging risk behaviors and encouraging good decision-making skills.

From internet safety and the impact of social media to drug and alcohol use and sexual activity, equipping students to make wise choices has lasting and positive impact.

And again, study after study demonstrates that religious participation and education make a big difference. Here are just a few examples:

- "Religious involvement is generally associated with greater wellbeing, less depression and anxiety, greater social support, and less substance abuse."[15]

- The National Center on Addiction and Substance Abuse at Columbia University reported that "rates of drug and alcohol abuse have been found to be significantly lower in those who are religious compared to their nonreligious counterparts."[16]

- One survey of studies, over half of which focused on teens, found that "the research is almost unanimous in reporting that religious persons are less likely to abuse alcohol or take illicit drugs."[17]

Religion and good character go hand in hand. From encouraging respectful behavior and avoiding negative or harmful ones, religion and religious education have a powerful, positive effect that protects and empowers students to live a safer, healthier life.

AREA OF IMPACT #2: MENTAL HEALTH

It is one of the scariest statistics in education today—1 in 5 children are dealing with some form of mental illness, and nearly 80 percent of those children won't receive appropriate treatment.[18]

This problem is significant, at all levels of education, and schools are trying admirably to address this health emergency. Religious education could be another powerful tool in that arsenal.

With only a few exceptions, decades of research have clearly demonstrated that religious participation effectively lowers rates of suicide as well as anxiety, depression and other mental disorders.

- "84% [of studies] found lower rates of suicide or more negative attitudes toward suicide among the more religious."[19]

"Research has shown that religion and spirituality are

Students often find real, measurable success when their academic studies are paired with religious education.

✦ generally associated with better mental health [as well as] lower levels of depressive symptoms, fewer symptoms of posttraumatic stress, fewer eating disorder symptoms, fewer negative symptoms in schizophrenia, less perceived stress, lower risk of suicide, and less personality disorder."[20]

✦ "Religion can 'serve to ease dread and anxiety, reduce personal and group tension and aggressiveness, allay fears, and moderate loneliness, depression, anomie, and/or feelings of entrapment and inferiority.'"[21]

Even better, religious participation also seems to have a direct correlation to positive mental health.

✦ "[Psychologists] not only were wrong to blame mental illness on religion but were doubly wrong for failing to realize that religiousness provides substantial protection against mental illness. It can even make people happier."[22]

✦ "Nearly 80% [of studies] found religious beliefs and practices consistently related to greater life satisfaction, happiness, positive affect, and higher morale."[23]

Amazingly, there doesn't seem to be any group for which religion does not benefit mental health. "Studies of subjects in different settings ... ethnic backgrounds ... age groups ... and locations ... find that religious involvement is related to better coping with stress and less depression, suicide, anxiety, and substance abuse."[24]

The research is abundantly clear. In the face of rising rates of mental illness among even the youngest school children, reinstalling religious education can reduce negative effects and increase positive effects on students' mental health.

A QUICK BREAK

EXPLAINING AWAY THE CONNECTION

"They're probably just good kids."

Some people think the connection is more about the students than about religion. That students who are more likely to be religious are also more likely to do better in school.[32] However, the "evidence [is] that these positive outcomes ... are not simply a reflection of "selection effects" [or] the likelihood that religious teens are also the kind of youth who would perform well in school."[33]

"It's just a family thing."

Or perhaps it is just family support that makes the difference? Again, no. A 2020 study of sibling pairs found that personal religiosity was a positive factor on GPA, college expectations, and education completed, separate from family influence. While good grades were somewhat connected to family support, the study found that long-term measures (college aspirations and degrees completed) were more connected to personal religiousness.[34]

Are you still with me?

I get really excited when I see just how easily we can demonstrate the measurable, positive impact of religion and religious education.

I hope you're seeing it and getting excited too.

Because our next section is one of the most significant in terms of education. Contrary to popular belief, religious involvement actually has a positive impact on students' academic performance.

AREA OF IMPACT #3: ACADEMIC ACHIEVEMENT

Students often find real, measurable success when their academic studies are paired with religious education. "It seems that religiosity instills values that when affirmed and reinforced, [create] an environment that motivates students to be successful academically."[25]

Religion can help students stay "on track" academically. Being on track means "maintaining an adequate GPA, keeping up with homework, maintaining progress through grades, getting along with classmates, avoiding disciplinary action, and refraining from skipping class."[26]

Other studies have found that "students who take the time to commit to spiritual activities enhance their ability to excel academically"[27] and those "who participated in religious activities and/or had spiritual beliefs had better academic performance."[28]

Rodney Stark agrees: "Religious students have a superior level of academic achievement, however it is measured."[29] He continues:

> Compared with less religious students, religious students
>
> ✦ Score higher on all standardized achievement tests.
>
> ✦ Get better grades.

Unexpected Impact   65

- ✦ Are more likely to do their homework.
- ✦ Are less likely to be expelled or suspended.
- ✦ Are less likely to drop out of school.[30]

Christian Smith sums it up this way: "After controlling for ... family and individual effects, a significant religious effect on academic achievement remains."[31]

At-Risk Advantage

This positive influence of religion on academics seems to be even stronger for at-risk and disadvantaged students.

Studies have shown that "as the level of poverty rises within the neighborhood, the relationship between church attendance and being on-track in school becomes more positive, indicating a uniquely protective influence of church attendance among youth in more impoverished neighborhoods."[35]

And according to Ivory Toldson, editor of *The Journal of Negro Education*, "Religious involvement shows especially positive relationships with achievement for students in lower-income neighborhoods than students in higher-income neighborhoods."[36]

This connection has been demonstrated in study after study for decades.

A 1996 study concluded that "religious socialization was related to educational attainment for younger blacks, regardless of whether they enjoyed the positive influence of a two-parent home or a residence outside the central city,"[37] a conclusion shared by Harvard economist Richard Freeman in his study on religion and academic achievement for "African-American male youth in high-poverty neighborhoods."[38]

A LIFEWISE

"Tidbit"

Many school administrators that we meet want to offer their students the opportunity to receive religious instruction and connect with the faith community, but they often feel their hands are tied. Recently, one inner-city elementary school principal shared with a LifeWise team member that she had been looking for a church that would come alongside the school to invest in her students. In our meeting, she was overjoyed to learn about the launch of a LifeWise Academy to serve her students.

Religion and religious education positively impact character, mental health and academic achievement.

Bridging the Achievement Gap

The research even indicates that religious education may help address the achievement gap that "exists on every measure of achievement: standardized test scores, grades, being held back a grade, and staying in school."[39]

Patrick Fagan noted religion's "wide-ranging capacity to boost the academic potential of young people, especially for those who need it most."[40]

And David Hodge found that, rather than struggling on standardized tests, Latino students in a released time program did equally well as their peers who did not attend the program.[41] Many other researchers have reported similar results.[42]

William Jeynes, a leading expert on the positive effects of religion on education, is adamant that religion does positively address the achievement gap.

"Of all the variables included ... religious faith [whether personal, school-based or a character-based curriculum] was the one that produced the largest effect size [on the achievement gap]."[43] It's significant enough that, according to Jeynes, "religious faith can reduce the achievement gap by more than 50%."[44]

AREA OF IMPACT #4: COMMUNITY INVOLVEMENT—THE HOLY GRAIL OF EDUCATION

Still tracking? I hope so, because we made it to the last point in the chapter. And for many schools, this one may be the most important of all.

Religion and religious education positively impact character, mental health and academic achievement, but they also correspond to positive and effective community involvement.

Administrators and teachers have long recognized the influence of community involvement on schools. "The positive impact of connecting community resources with student needs is well documented. In fact, community support of the educational process is considered one of the characteristics common to high-performing schools."[45]

So what does this have to do with religion? Local churches and church attenders often provide a powerful, positive community influence for many students.

Churches are highly committed to their communities. "[They] are often among the last institutions of civil society to leave and first to return to low-income urban neighborhoods and communities,"[46] making them a powerful "socializing agent" for students.[47]

And they provide a highly positive influence.

Churches can "create an 'umbrella of legitimacy' for youth" by creating "a place where social attitudes and behaviors, academic achievement, and future-oriented planning is valued and encouraged."[48]

And they "can [provide] the sorts of social and cultural capital rewarded by schools and teachers, and [promote] attitudes and practices conducive to positive educational outcomes."[49]

Simply put, when community groups, including religious groups and churches, invest in schools, positive outcomes result.

> Religion helps to reinforce the importance of staying in school, working hard to attain good grades, and achieving a diploma. ... Youth in church communities are motivated to excel (and behave properly, etc.) not simply by their own will, but by their connection to others who expect it.[50]

The NEA put it this way: "When schools, parents, families, and communities work together to support learning, students tend to earn higher grades, attend school more regularly, stay in school longer, and enroll in higher level programs."[51]

DID YOU START SKIMMING?

That was a lot. I get it. But I think it's valuable to see all the evidence laid out this way.

(I actually had even more info in this chapter that I chopped and moved to Appendix 2: "Even More Impact." For those who are interested in more, or who are just major nerds, flip there for extra goodness.)

The evidence is clear. When we reinstall religious education during school hours, schools and students benefit—in character, mental health, academic achievement and community involvement.

Most people know it. Researchers can prove it. I've seen it.

I hope that you can see it now, too. I hope you're beginning to see the value and benefits religious education could bring. But maybe you still find yourself hesitating.

In that case, let's push on to chapter 4, and hopefully, we can lock in the WHY of reinstalling religious education for you.

CHRISTIAN'S STORY

Scan to Watch Video

A LIFEWISE STORY
"Bethany and Her Son, Christian"

When the LifeWise flier arrived in the mail, Bethany Sanidad was surprised to learn that a Bible class was being offered for public school students during the school day. She remembered being somewhat involved in church when she was a child, but she and her husband had not yet exposed her son, Christian, to religion.

As Bethany considered the LifeWise description of "Bible-based character education," she thought, "Well, it can't hurt." So she signed Christian up.

Christian loved LifeWise Academy from the first day. He was brand new to it all; even the word *Bible* was unfamiliar. But he was excited and curious. He came home each day and told his mom about the Bible stories and how much he was learning.

"Without LifeWise Academy, I don't even know what our family would look like today."

After just a few weeks of class, Christian asked his LifeWise teacher if she would call his mother to invite his family to church. So she did.

Christian's mom accepted the invitation, and their entire family attended the following Sunday. They loved it.

Through Christian's enthusiasm for LifeWise, their family now attends church regularly.

Bethany recently said, "Without LifeWise Academy, I don't even know what our family would look like today."

CHAPTER 04

AN OBVIOUS CHOICE
WHY Religious Education Creates True Neutrality

When we reinstall religious education during the school day,

schools and students begin to thrive—in academics, in character, in mental health and through enhanced community support.

Of course, reinstalling spiritual instruction isn't some magic fix for every problem facing schools and students, but it really is the most simple, most powerful key that is currently missing. All we have to do is put it back.

But many people are still not convinced. Maybe *you* aren't convinced ... yet.

Some people are always going to be opposed to what we are suggesting. They view religion as a regressive relic of a primitive society. They believe we've evolved past it. So they don't tend to listen to the evidence. Thankfully, these individuals are the minority.

Most of the people I talk to about LifeWise Academy want to do whatever they can to help students. But they are a little hesitant. They ask things like, "Is having the Bible available during the school day even allowed? Aren't schools supposed to be neutral?"

And I get it. It feels like maybe we're breaking some sort of rule. But we aren't (more on that in Part 2). In fact, and this may come as a shock, neutrality is the very thing I'm actually arguing for. And it's exactly what we don't currently have.

Let me explain.

THE (SHORT) HISTORY OF NEUTRALITY

The idea that schools are supposed to be neutral is deeply ingrained in our culture. It's also fairly recent.

In chapter 1, we looked at the huge shift in education from 1850–1950. During those decades, as schools embraced science and secularism, "'neutrality in religion' became the accepted mode in the classroom."[1]

One of the earliest moves toward neutrality was in 1872, when the Ohio Supreme Court decided *Board of Education of the City of Cincinnati v. Minor*.

The Cincinnati Board of Education removed the Bible from the district's curriculum in order to "[defend] the rights of those who did not follow the Christian religion."[2] The decision was challenged by local families, but the Court ultimately upheld the Board's decision.

From then on, this new idea—that those who don't believe religious ideas shouldn't have to hear about them while at school—gradually spread. And they called it neutrality.

By the 1930s, the general consensus for public education was that, to be neutral, schools couldn't include religious texts, particularly the Bible, in the curriculum or allow religious activities such as prayer in the schools.

Eventually that assumption was codified by the U.S. Supreme Court as well. By the 1950s, character education was "phased out of public education [for] fear that teaching morality would be equated to the teaching of religion."[3]

According to some, we had finally arrived. Our public schools were now neutral, and that's where things needed to stay.

But they were wrong. We weren't anywhere near neutral. We still aren't.

FALSE NEUTRALITY

As I've outlined, public education has been through a major shift in its relation to religion, but it hasn't been a shift to neutrality.

Think about driving a car. We have three basic settings: Drive, Neutral and Reverse. We can shift between them at any point in order to move the vehicle where we want it to go.

Now consider education. The early American approach to public education assumed that, in the area of religion, we needed to be shifted into Drive. We should be actively teaching religion.

By the turn of the twentieth century, that assumption had shifted. Religion was now seen as irrelevant and unnecessary. The changes that were made, they claimed, shifted education into Neutral. But they didn't. We shifted into Reverse.

At the center of the issue is silence.

For over a hundred years, we've been told that being neutral means being silent. In this view, neutrality means not allowing anything religious in any form to encroach on school buildings, school-sponsored events, school curriculum or school hours.

Instead, schools must be silent about religion. Its place at the table and its message and voice are to be eliminated from education. And to do otherwise, we've been told, would violate the separation of church and state since (they claim) we'd be actively supporting religion through the public schools.

True neutrality cannot mean encouraging one idea and discouraging the other.

This view is why so many people hesitate about reinstalling religious education into the school day. But is this approach correct? Not at all.

Because silence *isn't* neutrality.

Eliminating the voice of an opposing side isn't being neutral. Proponents of the silence approach didn't find a middle ground; they didn't simply prevent active support of religion. Instead, they shifted education into Reverse, actively moving students away from religion.

And that's not true neutrality.

True neutrality cannot mean encouraging one idea and discouraging the other. Or encouraging all the ideas *except* that one. But that is exactly the approach public education takes.

Think about it. Every single day, our public education system comments on lots of things. That's the point of having a curriculum—to know what we'll be talking about. So we are not silent about history and math, peer pressure and food pyramids.

But, we're told, we must be silent on religion. Just religion. When it comes to the spiritual, schools actively discourage, root out and refuse to speak about it at all.

And yet, sending a child to school for thirty hours a week and teaching him a vast array of details and disciplines but never mentioning the spiritual is, in fact, teaching something about the spiritual—it teaches that it's *un*important. That it has no place. That it can (and even should) be ignored.[4]

And that is not neutral. That is actively discouraging religion. And even our students recognize that fact.

"Silence, quick dismissive comments, or avoidance of a given topic ... generally do not convey neutrality, but rather communicate distaste for a given topic. Most adolescents, in particular, will be wise

A LIFEWISE

"Tidbit"

Only a number of weeks after we launched our first LifeWise programs, we saw an effect of reinstalling religious instruction into the public school day that we hadn't anticipated. We started getting reports of families in neighboring school districts pulling their kids out of those districts to send them to where LifeWise was being offered. Soon we got a call from an administrator in one of those neighboring districts asking how soon we might be able to expand the program to serve his schools.

✦ ✦ ✦

enough to interpret such responses as negative."[5]

Silence is disagreement and discouragement, not neutrality. And public education has embodied this false neutrality for a hundred years. But it is possible to shift again. We can achieve true neutrality in the public schools.

A SPECIFIC EXAMPLE

In 2020, William Jeynes published research on prayer that showed a positive relationship between prayer and student outcomes. Kids who prayed did better in school from kindergarten to college. Given that you've already read chapter 3, this shouldn't come as a surprise.

In the conclusion of that study, however, Jeynes acknowledges that teachers need to remain neutral about prayer, but he says, "True neutrality means the educator *does not seek to change the child's present religious disposition.*"[6]

True neutrality is simply that: truly neutral. A child open to prayer is free to share her enthusiasm. A student with questions isn't discouraged, but encouraged "to seek out more information on the topic rather than inadvertently ... stifling the youth's curiosity by silence or avoiding the topic."[7]

A truly neutral space is not one that actively prevents or subtly discourages a topic of discussion, even religion. Instead, it leaves space for both sides, for and against, and openly acknowledges both when it is appropriate to discuss them.

That is a neutral approach. It can be done in any classroom, but it can also be done in public education as a whole.

And the mechanism for making that approach a reality is choice.[8]

THE POWER OF CHOICE

Everyone loves to have choices. Just think of all the M&M or Oreo options we have these days.

But in the world of public education, talking about "choice" can make people defensive. So let me be clear about a couple of things up front.

As I promised at the beginning of this book, there will be no soapbox about "school choice" here. We won't be discussing charter schools or the benefits of alternate approaches to public education. The word *voucher* will appear only in this sentence. You're welcome.

But I do want to state—clearly and for the record—that many parents want the option to reinstall religious education into the school day. I hear from them and meet them every day. They are the reason that LifeWise Academy is growing so rapidly.

Parents are not satisfied with the false neutrality of silence. According to The Heritage Foundation, "Parents rank moral and character development as one of the top three most important qualities in a school."[9] Families want more. They want to prioritize the moral and the spiritual. I am convinced they should have that option. How else can the public school be truly neutral?

But neutrality isn't the only reason choice is so valuable. Let me give you three more reasons why it's so critical to offer parents the choice of religious education for their children.

1. People don't want more choices; they want better choices.

Did you know that psychologists and researchers have actually studied what we choose and why we choose it? It's a whole field called the psychology of choice. And I mention it here because researchers have learned that we like the *idea* of choices, but don't actually manage them well.

With too many options, we quickly get overwhelmed and make a knee-jerk decision or no decision at all. What does work for most people, though, is to be offered curated ideas or a smaller number of personalized options. Then people move forward easily.[10]

The choice to reinstall religious education into the school day is that better, curated option.

Parents already have lots of educational options: public schools, private schools, charter schools, Christian schools, homeschooling and more. They can and do choose among the options based on what is best for their families.

In fact, the very existence of private Christian schools demonstrates how much parents want the option to include religious education. They're willing to pay thousands of dollars in tuition, on top of school taxes, to have the choice.

And that's the real key. Parents don't just want another choice. They want a better choice.[11] They want to find the best combination for their family and their students. And for many families, reinstalling religious education into the public school day offers exactly the curated option they've been looking for.

It combines the best of multiple options into one better-than option. And offering that kind of choice makes it easier for parents to find exactly what they're looking for and what they can support wholeheartedly.

So give them the better choice.

2. Choice allows for local expression.

For much of early American education, the community determined what education was offered to its children with little outside influence. In the last 150 years, the pendulum has swung so that outside influences now determine education, regardless of what the community would prefer.

Church members want to get involved in their local school districts, but feel shut out.

Now, pendulums will keep swinging, in history and social movements and education. So I'm not saying that we can or should lock in a "perfect" point on the spectrum. But I do think it's time for the local community to have a greater say, once again, in what education looks like *for that community*.[12]

Schools and school districts exist within a community. They have a context. And if that context wants more religious education during the school day *as an option* for their students, then it is their right to ask for it.

And they are, in fact, asking for it.

In 2020, I attended a meeting to present LifeWise to an interested community. They wanted to launch a program at the start of school in fall 2021, which would be a fast and difficult turnaround. Coming out of that meeting, however, multiple local farmers were nearly arguing for the honor of donating some land near the school for a LifeWise building.

These men wanted to be involved in offering this new and exciting option to families. They wanted to see the schools serve their community more effectively, and they saw in LifeWise a chance to do just that.

I've seen it over and over again. Church members want to get involved in their local districts, but feel shut out. Communities want to serve the schools in positive and effective ways, and they want the schools to be able to serve the needs of their families and students.

Reinstalling religious education into the school day allows both things to happen at the same time. So give the community what it wants—a choice to get involved.

3. Choice is as American as apple pie!

Not to get too cheesy here, but seriously, this is America, right?

We don't need flags, patriotic music or apple pie on the table (okay, maybe the pie would be good), but we do need to recognize that America has always valued choice. It's tied up with freedom and independence in American history and culture.

It is uniquely American to both offer and take advantage of all the opportunities that exist. We are a people who have historically been willing to offer a variety of paths forward and hesitant to restrict options except in the most dire of circumstances.

Families and communities are looking for the freedom to do what is best for their students, their families, their streets and their schools.

So let's give everyone the option they are clamoring for.

WHERE WE STAND

All right, so we've made it through Part 1: the WHY of reinstalling religious education into the public school day.

Here's the ground we've covered so far:

1. Religious instruction was at one time central to public education in America, but it has long since been removed.

2. Removing religious education has resulted in negative consequences by betraying education's fundamental purpose of creating well-rounded students prepared to thrive.

3. The benefits of religious instruction in the areas of character development, mental health, academic achievement and community involvement are clear and significant.

4. Giving parents the option of religious education for their children is the key to establishing true neutrality in our public schools and meets the needs of families.

So I hope you're now wondering if there is actually a way to do this amazing thing of reinstalling religious education.

And there absolutely is. That's Part 2.

In the following chapters, we'll explore the practical side of things. We will cover all the nitty-gritty details of the legal and practical issues and introduce you to LifeWise Academy in the process.

So turn the page. Let's keep going.

Putting It back!

PART

TWO

How

We're Reinstalling Religious Education
with LifeWise Academy

JULIE'S STORY

Scan to
Watch Video

A LIFEWISE STORY
"Julie and Her Grandma"

When her local elementary school closed its doors in 1996, Mary ended a forty-year ministry. For four decades, she had taught a Bible education program to the elementary students of Brownlow, including her own son.

Mary's granddaughter is Julie. Julie is a successful physician who was challenged by her grandmother's life in a powerful way.

When Mary passed away in 2013, the funeral was packed.

At one point in the service, the pastor asked those who were there to stand if they had come to faith in Jesus through the Bible education program that Julie's

In her grandmother's life, Julie saw the impact one lady who faithfully serves can make.

grandmother had maintained for those decades. Nearly two-thirds of the room stood.

Julie was astounded. And she decided, right then, that if she ever had the opportunity to do something like what her grandmother had done, she would be all in.

Seven years later, Julie heard about LifeWise Academy, and she jumped in with both feet. She is currently the LifeWise Director for her suburban district, and they launched in not just one elementary (the original plan), but in all five elementary buildings in their district in the fall of 2022! Her district's superintendent has encouraged them to expand to the middle school as well.

In her grandmother's life, Julie saw the impact one lady who faithfully serves students can make. And she is carrying on that legacy with LifeWise Academy.

CHAPTER 05

A NEW FIT THAT'S KIND OF OLD
HOW Religious Education Integrates Legally

There was a time when teachers used the McGuffey Reader and the Bible as their textbooks in one-room schoolhouses.

There was a day when Tim Stoller's grandmother opened class with a devotional lesson (see page 35) and teachers taught religion right before or after math.

We want to reinstall religious education into the public school day, but what worked back then isn't going to work today. Trying to repeat past methods would be like pulling an old pair of pants from the closet. No matter how much we wish they fit, they don't.

But what if there was a way to reinstall religious education that didn't put schools in a compromising position? What if there was a way that allowed for family choice? What if there was a clear path forward for every school, family and community?

Actually there is.

It's what I've been mentioning here and there for the first four chapters. It's called released time religious instruction. Released time is an entirely legal, amazingly practical way to reinstall religious education into the public school day. And in this chapter, I finally get to start showing you exactly how it fits.

But first, we probably need to address the elephant in the room. Because we haven't yet talked about the thing I get *a lot* of questions about—legality. People want to know if released time is even legal.

And the answer is an unequivocal yes. Let me show you why.

A BIT OF BACKSTORY

To start, let's make sure we're all on the same page.

The key legal issue here is the separation of church and state or the idea that the Constitution requires the state and religion to be completely separate.[1] It's called the establishment clause, and it comes from the First Amendment:

> Congress shall make no law respecting an establishment of religion, or prohibiting the free exercise thereof.

This doctrine, in its current interpretation, actually draws on the work of two influential men in early American history who wrote that there was (or should be) a wall—a separation—between government and the church.

The first was Roger Williams who founded Rhode Island back in 1635.[2]

The other, more familiar one was Thomas Jefferson. In fact, he in-

TO COIN A PHRASE:
The Men Behind the "Separation of Church and State"

Roger Williams

Banned from Boston for his views on religion and the state, Williams founded Providence, Rhode Island, with a unique and non-religious charter. When the leaders in Boston sought to take over Providence, he requested and received a charter that would keep his new colony separate. In his request, he warned of what would happen "when they have opened a gap in the hedge or wall of Separation between the Garden of the Church and the Wilderness [sic] of the world."[4]

Thomas Jefferson

For his entire political career, Jefferson stood firmly against the establishment of a state church. He considered the 1786 Virginia Statute for Religious Freedom one of his greatest legacies. In it, he argued that the freedom to worship without being forced to attend or pay taxes toward a state church is a "natural right of man." This bill was one of the "driving forces behind the religious clauses of the First Amendment ... ratified in 1791."[5]

spired the entire separation doctrine. In an 1802 letter, Jefferson wrote that "the whole American people ... declared that their legislature should 'make no law respecting an establishment of religion, or prohibiting the free exercise thereof,' thus building a wall between church and State."[3]

In the twentieth century, the Supreme Court turned Jefferson's phrase into legal doctrine in cases such as *Emerson v. Board of Education (1947)*, *McCollum v. Board of Education (1948)*, *Engel v. Vitale (1962)* and *Abington School District v. Schempp (1963)*.

CONSIDERING THE OPTIONS

As with previous topics, I'm not here to argue anything at all about the separation doctrine itself. Again, my reason for bringing it up is simply to point out that it exists and is part of the educational landscape.

Instead, since this chapter is about HOW to reinstall religious education, the bigger question we need to ask is, "How do we apply the separation of church and state AND reinstall religious education?"

In answering that question, people tend to lean toward two extremes.

Eliminators

The first extreme is what we'll call the Eliminators.

These folks want us to apply the separation doctrine very strictly. They want no overlap between public education and anything religious. They are to be totally separate. And public schools and teachers should have little or nothing to do with the Bible or prayer or religious activities of any kind during the school day. Period.

Now again, legally, separation is our goal. It's not a bad thing. But it's important that we're actually separating the two things and not just eliminating one or the other.

Separation puts two things in separate spaces but doesn't throw out either one. It's like sending my sons to separate rooms when they aren't getting along. I need them removed from each other, but I don't throw either one of them out of the house.

Separation is fine; elimination is not. And often, this first group tends toward the second, while claiming they're doing the first.

Conflaters

The second extreme takes the opposite approach; we'll call them the Conflaters. They don't want much, if any, separation to occur.

These folks want the Bible and prayer in the schools. They think the separation of church and state has nothing to do with the curriculum of a particular school, and they have no problem with teachers teaching a devotional lesson in the classroom.

(To be fair, allowing teachers to teach a devotional lesson during class hours is not necessarily bad. But it is a complicated issue. Do we want state employees teaching a particular religious view to students?)

Again, the issue is separation. The first group wants to put the ideas into two boxes, but throw one out entirely (elimination). This second group wants to put both ideas in one box with only a flimsy divider between them. And if the divider falls, no biggie.

Obviously, neither extreme sufficiently answers the question of how to reinstall religious education into the school day. We need *separation* without *elimination*. We need *integration* without conflation.

We need the LifeWise Way.

THE LIFEWISE WAY

The LifeWise Way is the released time model. School children are released from school during the school day to attend a religious class.

This path honors the separation doctrine perfectly. It's an entirely optional way for families to integrate religious education into their children's public education.

And, to be fair, it's not even new. LifeWise Academy is new, but released time is old. Vintage, even. It's like an old map that we never thought to pick up and follow to buried treasure. Like a Highlights hidden picture puzzle, it's the umbrella that's hiding in plain sight.

But it has been there, hidden away in a less-famous Supreme Court case from 1952, the perfect opportunity that we've missed all this time.

Let me tell you how it all came about.

ZORACH V. CLAUSON (1952)

What started as an attempt to further crack down on religion in public schools became, in the process, a road map to an incredible opportunity.

In 1948, an Illinois school district allowed religious teachers to come in and teach classes during the school day. A concerned resident sued, and the case made it to the Supreme Court in *McCollum v. Board of Education*. According to the Supreme Court, the practice of offering a Bible class was deemed unconstitutional because it was compulsory (though parents did give permission) and held on school property.

But in 1952, another religious program, this time in New York, was sued on the same grounds. Again, the plaintiffs appealed all the way to the Supreme Court, except this time, the Court decided 6–3 in favor of the religious program, not the plaintiffs. That decision was *Zorach v. Clauson*.

So why the change? Why, only four years later, did the Supreme Court seem to reach a different conclusion?

Two very significant differences existed between the 1948 and 1952 programs.

Like the Illinois program, the New York program was held during school hours, but it occurred off of school property and only with parental permission. Because of those differences, the Supreme Court declared that both free speech and the establishment clause were upheld, and the program was allowed to continue.

The only such outcome in nearly two decades, the 1952 decision legally allowed for a working relationship to be reestablished between public and religious education. "*Zorach* was the first clear statement by the Court that government should recognize and accommodate the religious beliefs of its citizens."[6]

And in doing so, they created a clear and legal path for religious education to be reinstalled into the school day. In the decision, they provided a three-pronged test, a simple map, that allows us to reinstall religious education through released time programs.

LEGAL RELIGIOUS EDUCATION

According to *Zorach v. Clauson*, students may be released from school (thus the name *released time*) during the school day for religious classes as long as the program follows three requirements:

1. Off school property.

Students must leave their school campus for the purpose of biblical or religious education. Classes may be held in a local community or church building willing to host the program or in a building converted specifically for the classes. As long as they do not meet on school property, though, the program is considered legal.

2. Privately funded.

No tax money may be used to fund a released time program. Denominations, community members or local churches may provide the money, curriculum and teachers, but no taxpayer money can

A LIFEWISE

"Tidbit"

When we say it seems like "no one" knows about released time, we mean it. Most superintendents and school board members we meet have never heard of released time, even when their district policies already address it specifically. One of our team members presented at a recent school board meeting and referred to the Ohio law about released time. In response, a board member asserted that we must be taking an unrelated law "out of context." She was then shown Section 3313.6022 of the Ohio Revised Code titled "Released Time Courses in Religious Instruction." Not long after, the board adopted a policy to allow for released time.

✦ ✦ ✦

be used for anything related to the program. The financial burden of the program must fall entirely outside the school's tax-funded budget. So the program can send home flyers through the school, for example, but the school wouldn't be able to print the flyers with paper, toner and a printer purchased by the school.

3. Voluntary (with parental permission).

In the mid-twentieth century, the Supreme Court decided in a number of cases that prayers, reading of religious texts and religion classes were basically compulsory, even when parents were given the option to opt out, because students are required to attend schools. Therefore, an off-site, community-funded program must still be entirely voluntary. Parents must opt their children *into* the program (not out of), and the classes must not interfere with students' regular academic classwork.

FILLING IN THE DETAILS

Of course, people tend to have a lot of questions about released time when I present the concept. So I think a quick Q&A will be the easiest way to address the most common ones.

Is released time different from teaching the Bible in school?

Yes. The Bible can already be taught in history or language arts classes as part of a public school curriculum. But that is not religious education. The Bible is not primarily a history or literature text. It is a spiritual and moral text. Released time focuses on the Bible's spiritual teachings, with historical or literary qualities being secondary. Rather than replace the academic study of religious texts, released time is the study of the Bible *specifically* as a religious text.

Doesn't released time mean schools will be promoting religion?

Not at all. As we saw in chapter 4, neutrality means that schools can neither encourage nor discourage participation in religious activities or classes. The school and district cannot create or require a released time program; it must come from the community. Therefore, offering the option shouldn't be construed as promoting religion. If allowing a released time program were the same as promoting it, then not allowing a program would, likewise, be considered discouraging it. Schools are free to cooperate with released time programs while neither encouraging nor discouraging participation.

Won't someone sue?

Well, it's possible. Anyone can sue for any reason. We can't stop that or those who wish to complain about released time programs. But the reality is that the legal case for released time is so clear that there is no loophole to be found. LifeWise Academy has already had a couple of interactions with a national organization that opposes religion in public schools, but nothing like a lawsuit has ever materialized since LifeWise is clearly within the legal guidelines.

What about other religious groups, like Satanists?

When I get this question (and I do), my go-to answer is, "What about them?" Any religious group can use this same roadmap to establish a program if they want to do so. There is no limit, and I wouldn't want to see any limits established. Our team is confident in the LifeWise program, and we trust parents to make decisions for their students.

As for those who might teach something I disagree with, fine. I have no concerns with other released time programs cropping up. The Bible can compete in the marketplace of ideas, so if other groups wish to establish competing groups, that only means we can offer more and better conversations to our students.

Of course, you may have other questions. For lots more information, check out the extended FAQ in Appendix 1.

A NEW OLD FIT

Released time is a legal and practical path for reinstalling religious education into the public school day. It's a perfect, if long-overlooked, opportunity because the LifeWise Way does four things:

- It honors all legal requirements. The kids literally leave the school to participate, so it's a beautiful, visible manifestation of the separation of church and state.

- It empowers parents to make an active choice for their children if they desire, while creating no significant negative consequences for those who choose not to be involved.

- It empowers students, schools and communities to experience the overwhelming benefits of religious instruction outlined in chapter 3 without expending the districts' financial or personnel resources.

- Most important of all, released time can provide students with that foundational piece, the moral-spiritual element that holds all the rest of their education together, to build a well-rounded thriving life.

This is an opportunity that is too good to pass up. And yet, if released time is so amazing (it is) and it's been around since 1952 (it has), how come no one's ever heard of it?

Good question. The answer is in the next chapter.

JESSICA'S STORY

Scan to Watch Video

A LIFEWISE STORY
"Jessica Brings Phil"

My friend Jessica gets the credit for bringing Phil Nofziger to his first meeting about LifeWise Academy in 2018.

Jessica worked in Van Wert and knew about the Cross Over the Hill released time program there. She lived about an hour away in Ayersville, where her kids attended school, and she wanted to bring LifeWise to her community.

Jessica wanted Phil and his wife, Robin, to meet me and hear about released time. The Nofzigers were members of the same church as Jessica, and Phil had just retired after 29 years as a public school administrator. He was a trusted voice.

Phil and Robin agreed to attend the meeting, but Phil, in particular, was skeptical. When he heard that the meeting was about removing students from schools

By the time we had gotten school approval, Phil had agreed to lead our very first LifeWise launch.

during the day for Bible class, all sorts of red flags went up in his principal's mind.

Another source of hesitation for Phil was that LifeWise didn't really exist yet. It was only an idea. It didn't even have a name. There was just some crazy former Ohio State Buckeye football player enthusiastically plugging released time as an old strategy that was somehow also the way of the future. It didn't sound promising.

But after one meeting, Phil was sold. Released time was a legitimate strategy. How had he never heard of it?

Phil became convinced that this was an opportunity he could not pass up. LifeWise dovetails his two passions—education and his faith—perfectly. And he was the ideal candidate to lead the charge: after 29 years as an administrator in the area, everyone knows him.

By the time we had gotten school approval, Phil had agreed to lead our very first LifeWise launch.

To be continued…

CHAPTER 06

70 YEARS IN THE WILDERNESS
HOW Released Time Has Survived

The day I spoke at the Van Wert building dedication in 2018

(see page 9), I was also invited to sit in on a board meeting. That day, the board asked me what has become the most compelling question I've ever heard.

I now call it "The Riddle." It goes like this: Why aren't more communities doing released time?

If released time is legal, and it clearly is (see chapter 5). If it is effective and impactful, which it clearly is (see chapter 3). And if the students and families love it, which they do—in Van Wert, over 95 percent of elementary students participate. If all of that is true, then why doesn't *every* community have one of these programs?

Communities can support at least one McDonald's, a library, youth sports of all kinds, a community center or YMCA and a variety of churches, so one would think that every community in America would also have a program like this to teach the Bible to their public school students.

But they don't. Very few released time programs exist. I'd been working full time with schools around the country for more than a decade before I even heard of released time.

It is definitely time to ask why. Why hasn't released time spread since the 1952 Supreme Court ruling? And what would it take to make it grow now?

The board challenged me to think about it. And I did. Actually, I couldn't stop thinking about it.

I had an idea that day about what released time could look like. But I also wasn't arrogant enough to think I'd really stumbled onto something totally new. Surely someone else had already done what I was imagining, right?

I made it my mission to find out. And that's why I like to call that day, "The day I stopped sleeping." (I'm only slightly kidding.)

I began to research released time. And I discovered two things.

First, a program like the one I was envisioning, one that could spread to every community, did not exist and, as far as I could tell, had never existed. And second, there were some really good reasons why.

BEFORE AND AFTER ZORACH

Released time programs existed even before the 1952 Supreme Court case, Zorach v. Clauson, established its three-pronged roadmap.

But the Zorach decision, which should have been a "win" for religious education, ultimately wasn't. Instead, we can see an important, and somewhat surprising, before-and-after pattern.

Before Zorach, there had been a steady increase in religious instruction programs. The very first one was in 1914 in Gary, Indiana.[1] And by the end of the 1940s, there were released time programs in 46 states.[2]

The Supreme Court actually researched these programs for the McCollum decision and found that "according to responsible figures almost 2,000,000 in some 2,200 communities participated in 'released time' programs during 1947."[3] In 1948–49, a quarter of the superintendents who responded to an NEA survey had a released time program in their district, serving about two million students.[4]

For nearly forty years, religious programs and released time programs spread throughout the country. But then the Supreme Court erected legal barriers against religious programs and religious activities in public schools.

After that, everything changed.

After McCollum in 1948, and despite the Zorach decision in 1952, the number of released time programs dropped by 12 percent across the nation.[5] Most of the programs that had existed before 1947 were not reinstated when Zorach was decided, and very few new programs were started to replace them.

After 1952, it was as if released time was immediately snuffed out. So what happened?

There are several theories about this stark before and after.

Most earlier released time programs were not likely in compliance with all three prongs the Supreme Court laid out in 1952. Many were happening on school campuses, and moving off campus presented significant logistical challenges. So lacking the time, personnel, money or church support to completely reinvent the programs to become compliant, their leaders chose to shutter them completely.

Another theory is that most people never heard of the *Zorach* decision or, if they did, didn't realize its implications. This was the only Supreme Court decision in favor of religious education in almost twenty years, and it could have simply been lost in the overall crackdown on religious education in public schools happening during those decades.

My personal theory has to do with timing. Released time was defined too early, before communities saw the need for it.

Basically, while the Supreme Court decisions took effect immediately, applying them into every district took much longer. If local schools or communities didn't really think the legal stuff was a big deal or thought it would never impact their region or their school, they may have dismissed the court cases as extreme.

By the time the legal crackdown on religion in schools hit them locally, the idea for released time was buried in the details of legal history. When communities finally saw the need, there was no practical way to discover the solution that had already been defined.

It's like a scientist in the 1850s writing a book that defines quantum mechanics. Even if someone read the book at the time (which wouldn't be likely), it wouldn't have been relevant yet. But over a hundred years later, when we've actually started studying quantum mechanics, no one would even know to find and read his book.

Of course, we really can't know exactly what caused such a major change. Whether it was any (or all) of these reasons, however, the end result was the same: the number of released time programs took a nosedive following *McCollum* and never recovered.

RELEASED TIME TODAY

That is not to say no released time programs exist now. They do.

Many small programs exist, run by pastors, retired teachers and community members, that have students walk or bus to a nearby church for a Bible lesson. But very few churches or groups have been willing or able to invest the time and money it takes to develop and sustain a program long term on a large scale.

Those that have maintained consistent released time programs over the years—particularly the Mormon church in Utah and some Catholic or Jewish communities—tend to have established infrastructure and strong support from a central church authority.[6] In general, though, the public school system is vastly underserved by released time programs.

Current estimates are that there are about 500 active released time programs in existence today, serving around 350,000 students.[7] And while investing in 350,000 students is a great thing, that number is only .7 percent of the 49.9 million public school students that are currently enrolled in the education system.[8]

It is also notable that many *good* released time programs exist.

As I said, there are many programs run by groups and individuals who have been using released time in powerful and positive ways over the years. Their work is changing lives. My friend Julie's grandma was one of those influencers for decades. Wherever they are, we applaud them.

We also applaud the advocacy groups who work alongside released time programs to create associations of independent programs or to offer support and legal advice. One of those groups, School Ministries Inc., helped craft a 2012 Ohio law on released time. As a program headquartered in Ohio, we are greatly indebted to their work. LifeWise may not even exist if it had not been for their efforts.

But all of this brings us back to The Riddle.

Because the question isn't "Why doesn't released time work?" It does work. We know it does. And it isn't "Why don't we have released time programs anymore?" We do.

The Riddle is, "Why hasn't released time exploded?" Despite the hard, caring work of many individuals, why has released time remained small scale?

We have the desire and opportunity. We have a legal path forward. We have many, many concerned and committed parents and community members. There are dozens of churches who would give nearly anything to see children back in their buildings.

Released time programs have not flourished in the last seventy years because there are significant barriers to entry.

So there has to be something else at play. Something has to have prevented released time from recovering from the catastrophic, mid-century drop.

And there is.

It's not actually very complicated. And it's not very surprising. In fact, it's entirely practical. Why doesn't every community have a released time program? Because of the barriers to entry.

BARRIERS TO ENTRY

Released time programs have not flourished in the last seventy years because there are significant barriers to entry. And when I say significant, I mean it. These barriers can seem impossible for most people or groups to overcome on their own.

On the surface, released time sounds so simple. Take kids off site, teach them the Bible and bring them back. Easy peasy, right? But it is much easier to say that sentence than to actually do it.

The reality is, it is hard to start a released time program and equally hard to keep it running. Let me give you some examples of the barriers to entry I'm talking about.

1. Funding

Every program has to figure out how to pay for itself. And full disclosure, there is no money to be made in released time.

So a released time program needs to get donations from churches or community members and get them regularly. It needs to pay for facilities, supplies, curriculum and sometimes staff. And that money now has to be managed. The program's directors will need to figure out banking, taxes, receipts, savings and the financial issues unique to nonprofits. Money is a very large barrier to entry.

2. Logistics

Every program needs a facility. Will it meet in an available space, or should it build or buy property? One meeting space may need transportation (a bus or van) with someone qualified to drive that vehicle. Other locations are close enough to walk to, but that requires chaperones to walk students to and from school.

Then there are personnel questions. Who will teach? Who will handle the administrative details? Who is responsible to make decisions when the questions or issues arise (and they will)? The logistics of a released time program require endless decisions on each issue, and this can become a barrier to entry.

3. School Relations

Released time programs exist to reinstall religious education into the public school day. That means every district, and sometimes every school, must be approached. Relationships must be built. Trust earned. Program leaders need to meet with school administrators, principals and school boards to get permission and hammer out the details of getting parental permission, scheduling classes, registering students, reporting attendance and the list goes on. Another barrier to entry.

4. Policies and Procedures

There are uncountable policies that must be put in place and procedures to be defined when starting a released time program. What safety procedures will be followed, during class as well as on the bus or the walk to and from the school? What about background checks? If the program doesn't have its own building, what policies or expectations will the church or community building require? What sort of discipline structure might you need, and how will it be enforced? These details, too, create a seemingly insurmountable barrier.

I could go on. There are marketing needs, curriculum questions, communication issues and more that all must be addressed. Each one is a barrier to entry. And most people, most communities simply don't have the tools they need to overcome those barriers and to bring to life in their community a released time program that works and works long term.

Starting and maintaining a released time program requires grit and an entrepreneurial spirit. It can feel a lot like facing down a wilderness of unknowns.

Which, actually, is my favorite metaphor for the process.

WANDERING IN THE WILDERNESS

As Americans, we understand the idea of pioneering our way through the wilderness. We learned about it in social studies classes. We've read books. Some of us played *Oregon Trail* and died of dysentery many times.

And that pioneer-style approach to released time has actually been the dominant approach since 1952. We have dozens of tiny programs all working toward the same goal, but always separately. Always reinventing the wheel. Always slogging through the barriers to entry one by one by one.

They are all navigating the wilderness.

In many ways, it's as if, in 1952, a new land was discovered. Few have seen this far-off land. But we do have a map. (Imagine a map of Middle Earth from *The Lord of The Rings*.)

On the left-hand side of this map is where nearly everyone lives, our current reality where students go to public schools but religion has no place there. We'll call it "Typical Land."

On the other side of the map is this foreign land, a beautiful, tropical paradise. There, public school students can be taught the Bible during school hours. We'll call it "Bible Education Land."

But these two places are separated by a vast wilderness. It's wild and untamed. The barriers to entry are like pits to avoid, rivers to cross, forests to navigate and mountains to climb.

Every so often, some brave, committed individual or group sets off through this wilderness, hacking down vines and fighting off wolves and navigating unfamiliar rivers until, finally, they reach the other side. They blaze a rough trail; they may leave signposts for those who come behind. But it's hard, mostly lonely work.

And like any journey to a new land, because so few make it, there is still much to do once they arrive. Sometimes, those who came before are willing to help, but there's no infrastructure in place; it all has to be built. Everything, from pitching a tent to getting food, must be done from scratch.

They made it. They're doing it. But each new arrival is still basically roughing it, pioneer-style.

This is the approach that has dominated released time programs for decades. Like a journey through the wilderness, few really get a program started. Like living in a land without infrastructure, the difficulty of sustaining a released time program is immense.

And that's the answer to The Riddle. That's why released time hasn't spread.

In a new world, if anything goes wrong or the intrepid explorer leaves, the entire expedition may fail. The same is true for building and maintaining a released time program. It's hard. And the last 70 years of released time proves it.

But there is hope.

WHAT IF?

What if we tamed the wilderness?

What if we cleared trees and built a multi-lane highway that makes the process of getting from Typical Land to Bible Education Land faster and easier?

What if, once there, we equipped each group with the initial tools and building materials they will need to quickly build stable, lasting homes and structures. What if we created infrastructure like a water treatment plant and a power grid they could connect to immediately?

It would take a lot. A lot of resources and time. But what if we made the investment?

It could be sustainable. It could be scalable. It could trigger a mass migration from Typical Land to Bible Education Land.

That's exactly what we've been cooking up with LifeWise Academy.

Let me tell you our story.

70 Years...

...in the wilderness...

The During School Hours Journey

School Relations River

The Pits of Policy

TYPICAL land

Bible Education LAND

Marketing Mountains

Fundraising Forest

Logistics Ledge

But what if...

The DURING SCHOOL HOURS Journey 1

School Relations River

The Pits of Policy

TYPICAL land

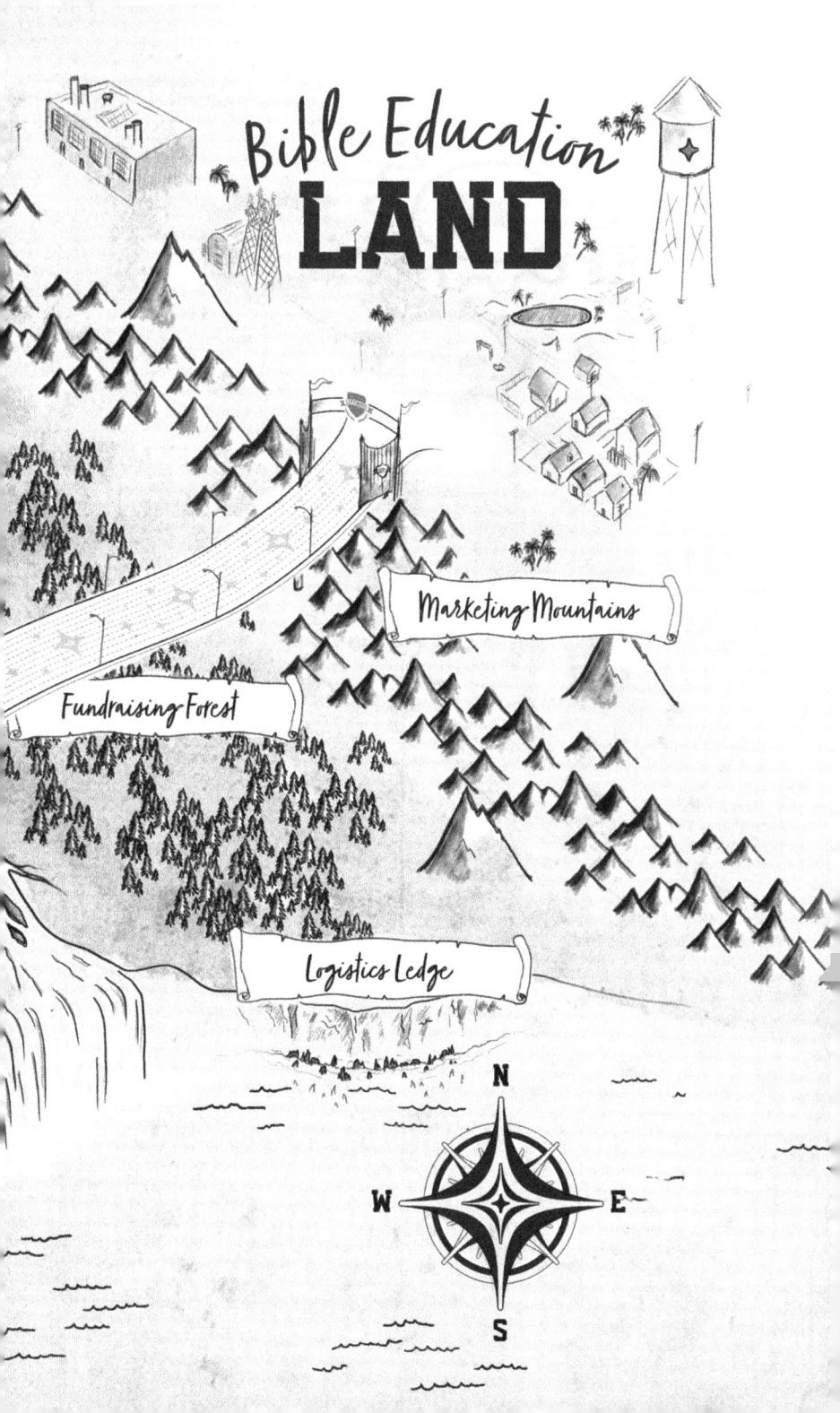

Bible Education LAND

Marketing Mountains

Fundraising Forest

Logistics Ledge

PHIL'S STORY

Scan to Watch Video

A LIFEWISE STORY
"Phil and the Modular"

Phil agreed to be our very first LifeWise Program Director.

He immediately set to work bringing a pilot program to Ayersville. (Fun fact: They are the Ayersville Pilots. No kidding.)

Of course, the process wasn't easy. Even with immense community support, there were big challenges.

The biggest was that while Phil had school approval, local community support and a piece of property next to the school, he did not have a classroom facility. When initial plans for a mobile classroom fell through just 90 days before the school year, Phil arranged a meeting with a local nonprofit called the Dream Center.

But Phil and
I only had
a Google
Drawing that
I'd personally
created on my
laptop.

Bill, G., and Rusty at the Dream Center said they could build a custom modular classroom in time for the school year if they got started immediately. All they needed, they said, were the architectural plans for the building. But Phil and I only had a Google Drawing that I'd personally created on my laptop. The guys said it was good enough.

The local team from the Dream Center dove in headfirst, got very creative, and worked long, crazy hours. And on the first day of school, our modular classroom was ready for students to come and learn the Bible. By the end of the school year more than 60 percent of Ayersville elementary students received a Bible class in the modular classroom.

Two years after launching the Ayersville program, Phil launched a second program in a much larger school district nearby. And by the end of the first semester, 800 of 1,000 students had enrolled!

Phil's input and influence is having a profound impact on his community. He once told me, "I have tried to work hard all my life, but my role in LifeWise is the most rewarding job I have ever done."

✦ ✨ ✦

CHAPTER 07

CRAFTING THE RIGHT TOOL *Part #1*
HOW LifeWise Academy Was Born

I'm sure you've heard the Thomas Edison quote about failure. Turns out he really said it.

One day, when a colleague asked if he was discouraged by having gotten no results from an experiment, Edison said something like, "I have gotten a lot of results. I know several thousand things that won't work."[1]

As Edison knew, and most of us have learned, creating something is hard work. It's easy to have a flash of inspiration, say wedding vows or decide to start a business. It's always a lot more complicated to flesh out that bolt of inspiration into something real and workable.

Recognizing a problem exists is easy. Creating the right tool to solve a particular problem is not.

But it can be done—in life, marriage and even in released time religious instruction. I won't attempt to give you advice on the first two. But I am very excited to tell you all about the last one.

COTH BUILDING
(Pre-2018)

And while I could describe it in nauseating (**and probably boring**) detail, I'm not going to do that. Instead, I'm going to tell you the story of LifeWise Academy. And if it sounds crazy at times, don't worry. It's all true, and it still blows my mind every time I tell it.

So here we go.

Once upon a time ... (I've always wanted to write that in a book.)

THE FORERUNNER (PRE-2018)

This book began with the story of the building dedication in Van Wert and how I drove home that day totally inspired by what I'd seen, what I needed to find out and just how big the possibilities were. I started dreaming and praying about all that God might do through released time.

But that is not actually the start of our story.

The story starts back in 2012 when a group led by the Putnam Family, Tim and Kari Stoller, and a few other individuals set out on the journey (through the wilderness) to start a released time program in Van Wert. They called it Cross Over the Hill (COTH).

Van Wert City Schools had just built a new elementary school on the outskirts of town, so the local COTH team went door to door, asking adjacent homeowners if they had any interest in selling their homes. Sure enough, the home closest to the school's front door

COTH VOLUNTEER
(Pre-2018)

COTH CLASS
(Pre-2018)

was available, so the Putmans and Stollers quickly raised the money to purchase and renovate the structure into a two-classroom facility.

The school administration was able to arrange the elementary schedule in such a way that COTH was incorporated into the "specials" rotation. In the same way that students receive art, music, library and gym once each week on a rotation, students would also have an opportunity to attend COTH weekly, with parental permission. Two classrooms at a time would be released. Rotating through the full number of classrooms would take three and a half days each week. It was a big undertaking to staff and prepare for the 2012 school year, but the COTH team was up for the challenge.

The team estimated that 30 percent of local students attended church, so they assumed their enrollment would be comparable. They were wrong. In the first year, 60 percent of students enrolled, and by year three, their enrollment reached 95 percent of Van Wert Elementary School students!

The work of COTH had an amazing impact in the community. But students wanted more. As they advanced out of elementary school, students started asking why they couldn't also attend COTH in middle school. So in 2016, the COTH team bought property beside Van Wert MS/HS and built their brand new, state-of-the-art educational facility for middle and high school classes.

But at some point it clicks. Their jaws drop and their eyes light up and they get it.

NEW COTH BUILDING
(2018)

THE RIDDLE (2018)

Somewhere along the way my sister, **Sara,** joined the COTH board. I'll admit that it's a bit embarrassing to point out that my sister was on the board for quite a while before I even understood the amazing opportunity of released time that was right under my nose.

Part of that was probably me being dumb. But knowing what I know now, my being slow on the uptake is actually pretty typical.

Over the past few years, I've noticed that it takes most people a while to "get" released time. We have to repeat the phrase "during school hours" and repeat it some more (hence the title of this book) and then answer a bunch of questions before people understand.

But at some point it clicks. Their jaws drop and their eyes light up and they get it. And that jaw-drop moment is really one of my favorite parts of my whole job.

But back to the LifeWise story.

Sara told me that the COTH board wanted me to speak at their building dedication ceremony. In fact she shared that I was their second choice to speak. They had first sent a request via email to the sitting U.S. Vice President, Mike Pence. When he didn't respond, they moved down their list of desired speakers to me.

To hammer out the speaking engagement details, Sara connected me with Tim Stoller (you met him in the story on page 34). Tim and

COTH MIDDLE SCHOOL STUDENTS
(2018)

I shared the stage at the dedication. In his speech he described the work COTH was doing as dropping a large rock in a lake. It will send out ripples throughout the country, he said. And he was right. Tim effectively dropped a large rock into my world that day when he posed the question, "Why doesn't every community have one of these?"

As I said already, I was immediately hooked.

On the two-hour drive home from Van Wert that day, the vision for a released time program popped into my head fully formed (though it didn't yet have a name). I thought through all I had learned and seen that day, and it all coalesced into one clear thought:

We have to "McDonald's" this thing.

That's how we would spread released time. It was our very best shot. And while I didn't know exactly what that meant at the time, the ideas were clear.

In my vision, this program would become a household name, a recognizable brand. It would be like YMCA or McDonald's: every community should have one. And it would have to be just right to engage educators and students—something I had learned from speaking in public schools for over a decade.

And from day one, on that car ride home, *just right* was already defined by a list of six things that were non-negotiable for this new venture. They later became our LifeWise Pledge.

COTH STUDENT READING THE BIBLE
(2018)

This program would be:

1. **Gospel-centered:** It must be genuinely on mission for the gospel, or it wasn't worth doing, and it wouldn't mobilize Christians.

2. **Character-focused:** It had to meet the felt needs of schools by addressing character education, mental health and academic performance.

3. **Local Church-driven:** This program shouldn't replace or displace local church efforts, but simply equip local churches.

4. **Plug and Play:** It would need to remove as many barriers as possible so no community ever has to reinvent the wheel again. It should build a highway through the wilderness and infrastructure in the new world.

5. **For the Nation:** Certainly, we would aim to see it in every place. The Supreme Court had already ruled, so why not have it coast to coast? But it also had to work in every context. Rural, urban, small town, big city, suburbs—the program had to serve every community.

6. **Excellent:** For this to work, there was no doing it halfway. We would need to be able to compete in the marketplace of ideas, programs and resources. Other ministry efforts may have small vision, shoestring budgets and fly under the radar. But we represent the King of the Universe. The country needs this, so we have to be all in. It has to be done big.

So we had a wild, crazy idea. But surely someone else had already thought of it, right?

THE BIG IDEA
(2018)

It was crazy, this idea. It was mind-boggling and completely unrealistic.

I envisioned that it would be, to use my favorite analogy, like blowing up the Death Star. From day one, I knew this project was like the rebel attack on the moon-sized space station in *Star Wars: A New Hope*. A thousand ships can fire at this project all day and night, and nothing big will happen (seventy years of attempts). But if, by God's grace, our little squadron can hit one very tiny bullseye—the Death Star thermal exhaust port[2]—if we do this just right, the whole thing could very well blow.

ANSWERING THE RIDDLE (2018, CONTINUED)

So we had a wild, crazy idea. But surely someone else had already thought of it, right?

Wrong.

As I shared in chapter 6, I did some research, and honestly, I couldn't find much. At least not anything that was really booming. Nothing that matched my vision. Perhaps there is something out there that I never uncovered. But if I couldn't find it, it seemed unlikely it would be effective in the way I was dreaming.

So that raised an important question: Was the idea off base? I sought counsel from several sources. Three are particularly memorable.

NAME AND LOGO DRAFT 1
(2018)

Advice Round 1 - Tim

I took the idea back to Tim Stoller on the COTH board. He loved the concept. It was exactly in line with his vision and what he'd been praying about for years. He was ready to dive in and start. I, however, thought we needed to pass these ideas off to someone more capable.

At one point, I said something like, "Wouldn't it be great if we could find an organization that's committed to the gospel, pursues excellence and has experience working with public schools? We could encourage them to take on this project."

Tim looked at me like I'd missed something very obvious. "Joel," he said, "you just described your organization. You guys have the experience working with schools. You've successfully launched a nonprofit and grown a team. You already have the ideas, and we can hire the team to make it happen. You should do this. I'll help fund it."

Oh. Well, when you put it like that, it was obvious. But I know Tim, and he's always ready to jump at just about any opportunity. That's one of the things that makes him so great. I decided I needed to ask some others.

Advice Round 2 - The Experts

So I took my idea to two people who had been in released time ministry for many years. They support released time programs

NAME AND LOGO DRAFT 2
(2018)

FINAL NAME AND LOGO
(2018)

around the state and country with encouragement, resources and advice, so I knew they would be an incredible source of wisdom and knowledge.

We set up a lunch meeting at a Bob Evans. I was excited to share my vision, and I was confident they would absolutely love the ideas.

They did not.

They were super nice about it, but ultimately told me the concept was a bad idea. It would never work. Communities wouldn't want something plug and play, they said. There's too much risk with a large organization, they warned.

To be fair, I'm sure my ideas sounded half baked. They were likely wondering *Who is this motivational speaker with zero experience in released time who thinks he has solutions?*

Still, they could sense I wasn't completely convinced by their reasoning, and at the end of the conversation, they assured me they would be supportive of whatever direction we chose.

Advice Round 3 - Barb

The church I attend possesses an invaluable treasure; her name is Barb Witt. Barb leads our church's children's ministry. She has the energy of a 7-year-old, the wisdom of a 300-year-old and the professional productivity capacity of a Fortune 500 CEO.

A LIFEWISE
"Tidbit"

Early in the process, we stumbled into the perfect curriculum. Through an unexpected sequence of people connecting us to other people, we were able to sign a licensing agreement with The Gospel Project to create the LifeWise curriculum. It is truly exciting. Students study through the entire Bible, Genesis through Revelation, over the course of five years. Every lesson focuses on the "head, heart, hands" approach. First we examine the information of the biblical text (head). Then we consider how it fits into God's overarching plan of redemption, the gospel of Jesus (heart). Finally, we discuss how this message transforms our lives (hands).

✦ ✦ ✦

LIFEWISE LAUNCH BANQUET
(2019)

Don't believe me? Consider this. She and her team write our church's Vacation Bible School curriculum each year—curriculum that is then published the following year by a major international ministry and distributed to thousands of churches in a variety of languages around the globe. Yep. Barb is legit.

So I took the idea to Barb. I sat with her in our church office conference room. I laid out the vision as well as the feedback I had received so far.

Barb's response was simple and matter of fact. "You have to do this. You don't have a choice."

She was right. Who was I kidding with all this "deciding whether or not to move forward" stuff? I already knew I was compelled. It was time to stop talking about it and do it.

As we concluded the meeting, Barb added one final piece of advice. "Joel, you need to make this good. It needs to work everywhere."

It was exactly the approach I thought would be necessary, but having Barb affirm it removed my last bit of hesitation. I didn't know what story the Lord was writing, but I did know we had to give it a shot. And so our team got to work.

PROOF OF CONCEPT (2019)

It was time to get some things down on paper.

LIFEWISE
AYERSVILLE

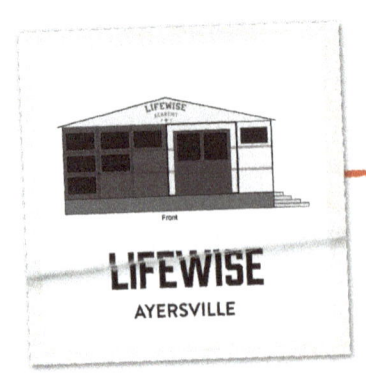

MODULAR CLASSROOM GOOGLE SKETCH
(2019)

In the office, we started hashing out our big picture philosophy (which turned into the six-point LifeWise Pledge). We created a first list of the resources, systems and services the central office would provide each LifeWise program to address barriers and serve as their infrastructure. And we honed our brand messaging.

But we also needed money. The initial goal was $500,000 to hire some staff and invest in the resources and systems we needed to get our dream off the ground. And it seemed, at the very least, unlikely.

I'd been running a nonprofit ministry for over a decade, and we had a decent donor base, but almost all our donations were small. Our typical gift is only $20 a month. How were we going to raise a half million dollars quickly?

But, growing up, my father had taught me, "List your work and work your list." So I applied that principal to fundraising.

I started contacting some key people in my network. And I pitched them … an idea. Really, at that point, we were vision casting, painting a picture of what *would be* possible if we could pull together the seed money. And it worked.

They caught the vision, and the money was pledged in a matter of months.

Looking back now, it seems kind of crazy. I was basically saying, "We've got this idea. We know it hasn't really worked for like seven-

UNDER CONSTRUCTION
(2019)

PHIL AND THE FINISHED CLASSROOM
(2019)

ty years, but we think we can do it!" And people gave: time, talent, treasure were all committed based on a vision of something that didn't even exist yet.

Last, we held some initial meetings with local communities. Basically, we needed some guinea pigs to try out our vision in reality. It was at one of those meetings that we connected with Phil Nofziger, and the Ayersville pilot was born.

Our second Proof of Concept program came to us from the other side of the state. Cindy Massie had heard of released time, but didn't know how to get started in her rural community on her own. She, too, quickly signed on to pursue a local launch.

Cindy and I met with an administrator at her local school in spring of 2019. Neither Cindy nor I had ever run a released time program before. But there we were, assuring this principal that all would be well. We were confident, even if we hadn't figured out all the details yet. And the school granted us approval on the spot!

Which meant we now had plans, funds, and pilot locations. All that was left was to bring the thing into reality. But, as always, the jump from drawing board to reality was not a smooth one.

We had to figure out everything as we went. We nailed down a policy manual. We licensed the curriculum. There were materials to create, like permission slips and signage, and a thousand other details.

Crafting the Right Tool (Part 1)

By the end of that first school year, both programs were serving over 60 percent of their local schools.

COTH REBRANDS TO LIFEWISE, TIM AND ME WITH THE NEW SIGN
(2019)

And with every system, process and resource we created, our team was focused on two things. One—this had to be done with excellence. No cutting corners. We knew that we had a tiny target, like the Death Star thermal exhaust port, but it was non-negotiable. And two—it had to be replicable. Everything had to scale up easily. Every new topic required us to ask "How will we do *this* times five, ten, twenty?"

And by God's grace, when the first day of school came in fall 2019, two LifeWise Academies went live on opposite sides of the state of Ohio. By the end of that first school year, both programs were serving over 60 percent of their local schools.

Best of all, the stories of impact and changed lives started rolling in. We were blown away. This thing could really work.

And in a powerful flourish that cemented our Proof of Concept phase, midway through that school year, the board of COTH in Van Wert voted to rebrand and restructure to become an official LifeWise Academy. They had been supportive from the beginning, wanting to see how these new ideas developed. But at the semester break, they moved to become more than just our forerunner and inspiration. They were now our flagship program.

Of course, I still wasn't sleeping much. The fact that LifeWise was working meant there was much more to do!

Now we had to blow this thing up.

Crafting the Right Tool (Part 1)

COLIN'S STORY

Scan to Watch Video

A LIFEWISE STORY
"Colin and the Zoom Call"

We hired Colin Heasley to be LifeWise Academy's very first Launch Coach.

It's a title we made up for a position we made up because I couldn't figure out a way to multiply myself. There were simply too many communities who were looking to start the launch process. I needed help. I needed Colin.

He spent several weeks with me in meetings and presentations, learning to do this incredibly important job of inspiring and equipping communities to launch a LifeWise program. Soon, he was ready to lead the meetings himself. And he did great.

Except for one thing. It soon became apparent there wasn't enough of Colin to go around either. And since neither of us could multiply ourselves, once again, we had to think outside the box.

For our launch meetings, we just have to be live and accessible. So we decided to try Zoom.

So we asked, "Why do we need to be in person?" Turns out, we didn't. For our launch meetings, we just have to be live and accessible. So we decided to try Zoom.

The bulk of the preparation for this new venture fell to Colin. He was overwhelmed and nervous. This was a big deal, with lots of moving parts, and a huge potential to fail.

Would the tech work? Would people show up for a meeting even if he wasn't there in person? If he messed up or people got confused, his mistakes would also be multiplied.

It was a lot for Colin, who is one of the most genuinely likable guys ever. But he dove in. And it worked.

Over the last few years, we've had dozens of virtual "Kickoff Meetings" with communities that are launching LifeWise in their schools, including one meeting that was attended by nearly twenty communities across four states.

Now I call Colin our "Launch Coach Head Coach" (it's another made-up title) because he's leading a team of Launch Coaches who are helping communities all over the country to launch LifeWise programs to make a huge impact in the lives of students.

✦ ✦ ✦

CHAPTER 08

CRAFTING THE RIGHT TOOL *Part #2*
HOW LifeWise Academy Started to Blow Up *(in a Good Way)*

As soon as we launched our two pilot programs, we began working on launch sites for fall 2020.

To do that, we started dissecting our first launches in minute detail.

We looked at what had worked and asked why it had worked. We looked for the critical elements that could be refined and repeated. And we dissected how we could build on those successes, make them even more intuitive.

On top of that, we were honest about what hadn't worked. Obviously, I skipped over those details in the last chapter, but that doesn't mean we got it all right. Far from it. We made mistakes all the way through the process. But instead of letting them derail us, we used them as jumping-off points for our next round.

And that's where we'll pick up the LifeWise story.

We recognized that there seemed to be a three-phase launch process, which we later broke down into ten steps.

NAILING THINGS DOWN

Since we now had our Proof of Concept phase, we began to work with other communities on potential programs, and we started to see patterns develop. We recognized that there seemed to be a three-phase launch process, which we later broke down into ten steps.

The Interest Phase

Early on, it became clear that one non-negotiable was that every program had to be community driven. LifeWise couldn't just be an agreement between our home office and the schools. It had to be grassroots. So we created the Community Interest List, a petition of sorts for each community. They had to collect a minimum of fifty names to get started. The Community Interest List shows our team that the community will support the program, shows the school that the community really wants it to happen and becomes the initial database for local leaders, volunteers, and donors.

The Planning/Approval Phase

After establishing that there is adequate interest, the local community forms a steering committee, representing various churches, which works with our staff to create a plan for that district and those schools. That plan is then presented to school officials for approval and coordination.

The Execution Phase

Once the plan is approved, it's time to execute it. Over time, we developed a t-minus plan that communities could follow step by step in the months and weeks leading up to launch.

In late 2019 we also began solidifying our Five L's of LifeWise Operations: Leadership, Location, Logistics, Loot and Language. Many of the nerdy details about these alliterative bad boys, which cover the day-to-day operations needed to maintain a local LifeWise program, are on (pages 164-165). (As good, sermon-loving Christians, we made sure they all started with the same letter.)

LAUNCH A LIFEWISE

10 Steps to Launch a LifeWise

PLANNING *Phase*

6. OBTAIN SCHOOL APPROVAL

5. DRAFT A PLAN

4. FORM A STEERING COMMITTEE

3. JOIN A KICKOFF MEETING

2. RAISE $500

INTEREST *Phase*

1. COLLECT 50 SIGNATURES

TRAIN YOUR TEAM

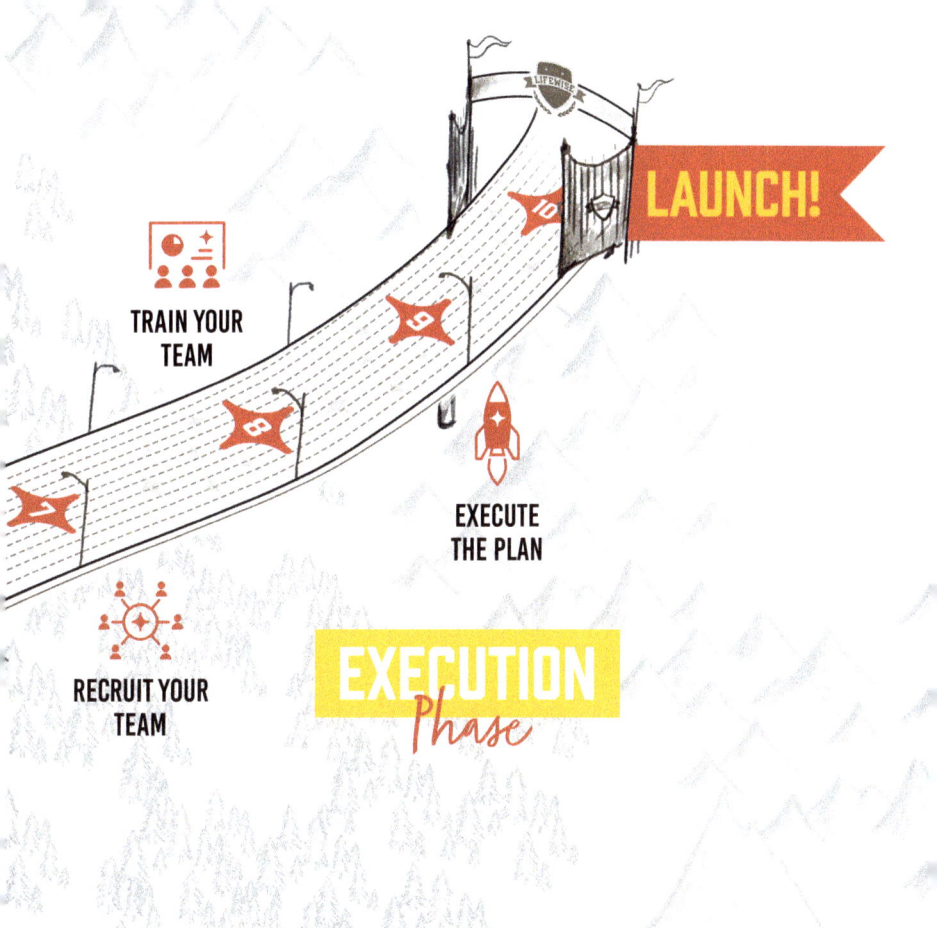

RECRUIT YOUR TEAM

EXECUTE THE PLAN

LAUNCH!

EXECUTION *Phase*

Scan to Watch Video

10

THE FIVE L'S OF OPERATION

LEADERSHIP

The people element, specifically the doers. The Leadership principle focuses on identifying, recruiting and training **Leadership Board members**, **Program Directors**, **teachers** and **volunteers** who will ensure the program runs smoothly.

LANGUAGE

The communication element. Through its connection with local schools and churches, LifeWise Academy seeks to connect with very different populations. This principle establishes clear guidelines for intentional and effective communication through an active prayer team, community outreach and well-crafted, public-facing messaging.

LOOT

The financial component. This principle comprises **fundraising**, budgeting and accounting, as well as all other **financial details**. LifeWise teams are encouraged to be excited and bold when raising funds: fundraising is biblical, and this is a vision worth sharing.

Scan to Watch Video

LOCATION

The **facility** and **transportation** needs for each community's program. Every LifeWise program must have an off-campus location where classes meet. Transportation for the students may need to be provided as well. It is imperative that facilities and vehicles are an excellent and visible representation of the LifeWise program.

LOGISTICS

The local **policies** and the **relationship between the LifeWise program and the school**. Any detail, from obtaining school approval to working with school officials for class schedules and **enrollment** requirements (such as permission slips or tracking attendance), is addressed here.

LIFEWISE PAYNE
(2020)

LifeWise Academy was well on its way. And it was at this point that things got really interesting. Because 2020 was about to come crashing down.

Which is why we call the next year ...

GOING VIRAL (2020)

(Get it? Too soon? Sorry. That joke is made in bad taste. Or perhaps we should say it's made in "no taste"! I'll be here all week.)

Obviously, we didn't get far into 2020 before things shifted. Fast.

Along with the rest of the world, March 2020 threw us for a huge loop. A pandemic? Six months after our first launches? Great. Just great.

We scrambled to create online tools and resources for our students who were now stuck at home. But even more, we scrambled to grasp exactly what all of this upheaval meant for the future of LifeWise Academy.

When would schools reopen? Would they still be willing to have conversations about released time? Would LifeWise need to skip a year of launches? Would we have the funds and the continued interest to weather this storm? Or would all of this spell an early end to our plans?

LIFEWISE GROVER HILL
(2020)

LIFEWISE STUDENT
(2020)

The questions seemed overwhelming at the time. But even as many schools closed their doors and many more nonprofits, especially those working with schools, struggled to keep their doors open, we survived the storm. In fact—and we are beyond grateful to God for this—LifeWise grew in spite of the storm.

All of our existing schools continued with LifeWise in the fall of 2020. And against all odds, we opened in not one, but *three* new school buildings across two school districts that fall. Both were significant, but for different reasons.

Wayne Trace Schools

One community that followed through with their LifeWise launch in spite of the pandemic is the Wayne Trace community. Let me tell you—these people don't mess around. They do all things with intentionality and excellence.

Wayne Trace has two elementary schools in their district, so I suggested they start with just one. Nope, they wanted to open both simultaneously to ensure equity between the buildings.

And then, one day, the local team called me and said they bought two pieces of property. "I'm sorry, what was that?" I replied.

Sure enough, a few of the guys had thrown their money together to buy a couple pieces of real estate, one beside each school. They immediately renovated one of the properties, a former two-car garage, and it is absolutely stunning. (And we all agree the biggest

A LIFEWISE

"Tidbit"

During the initial weeks of Covid lockdowns, school, church and community leaders weren't interested in working on future LifeWise plans. It was totally understandable. But our team wanted to make the most of our time. So what did we do? We looked up every single Ohio elementary school with the satellite view in Google Maps and used the distance measuring tool to see how close (in feet) the nearest church is to each school. We discovered that of the 1,400 elementary schools in the state of Ohio, 285 of them have a church within 1,000 feet—what we call walking distance. (And when I say "we" did this work, I mean Andrea did it. Thanks Andrea!)

✦ ✦ ✦

FIRST LIFEWISE SHUTTLE IN PANDORA, OH
(2020)

improvement was the change in smell. The previous owner must have owned a hundred cats.)

Pandora-Gilboa Schools

In Pandora, we achieved another first: we deployed our first LifeWise shuttle!

The church facility where we decided to hold classes sits adjacent to the school but just beyond walking distance. Until Pandora, we had hesitated to use any kind of vehicle for transportation, choosing instead to find or create an adjacent, walkable property. But then we realized that kids use buses for school every day, so we bought a shuttle, and it has worked out beautifully in every place we've used one. Today, about half of our programs use shuttles of some kind.

So despite the pandemic and all the resulting questions, by the end of 2020, we were serving eight school buildings across five school districts, with each program seeing a participation above 60 percent of their eligible students.

We started feeling inspired.

What if, we thought, *we dream really big? What if we set a goal to serve 25 schools by 2025. That'll really be pushing the envelope.*

It seemed like we had a great idea for our next chapter, but God had other (better) plans …

FIRST SUBURBAN PROGRAM
(2021)

MULTIPLICATION (2021)

We crossed into January and February of 2021, and the only word I have for that time is growth. And not just a trickle. In 2021, things really started to snowball for LifeWise Academy.

As more and more schools opened their doors again, more and more people wanted to learn about LifeWise. People in communities all over started Community Interest Lists and began working through the launch steps.

The LifeWise team grew too, trying to keep pace with this snowball effect, but we were simply unable to do everything one-to-one any more. We realized we needed to further systematize, further simplify.

We needed to start batching.

So we did. We leaned into the Zoom revolution (thank you, Covid?) and brought multiple communities together to train at the same time. We eliminated the use of Google Forms for our Community Interest Lists and hired web developers to build a list for every district in the country onto our website.

And still, things just kept multiplying.

In 2021, we launched 28 additional schools for a total of 36 schools across 27 school districts.

A LIFEWISE

"Tidbit"

Vince Coleman (you met him on page 50) joined our team in the fall of 2020 to lead the charge in bringing LifeWise to the greater Columbus (Ohio) area, especially the inner city. One of our priorities to see this through has been prayer. For more than two years, Vince and I, along with a few other men, have been meeting to pray for the Columbus area every Monday morning at 6 a.m. We are regularly seeing the answers to those prayers. If you had asked me two years ago to make a list of the five school districts in Central Ohio where it would be the most challenging to establish a LifeWise and then compare that list to where LifeWise exists today, you would see active programs in all five of those districts. I am thankful for Vince and the men who have been leading this effort with prayer.

✦ ✦ ✦

28 NEW SCHOOLS IN 2021

And we saw even more firsts. We launched our first program in Indiana (also our first program outside of Ohio). And we launched both of our first urban and suburban programs.

And in the middle of it all, hundreds more communities started to voice interest through the Community Interest Lists on the LifeWise website. Enthusiasm for what LifeWise was offering grew continuously.

Which prompted us to rethink our original "big" goal.

We thought 25 schools in five years was dreaming big, but in that second year alone, we grew 4.5 times to serve 36 schools. What if the Lord continued to open doors like this? What if next year, we got 2.5 times bigger? Then 2 times? Then 1.75 times? Just how fast might this scale?

We looked at the paper with our rough calculations, eyes wide. If those rates held, **we could be serving *one thousand* schools by 2026.**

And because we believe in the opportunity that LifeWise Academy represents and in seeing just how big of an impact God might make through it, we tossed out our original five-year goal and hung this bigger one, with two extra digits, in its place.

And then we got back to work. Because to reach this new goal, we had a lot of systems to build, training to do, resources to create and money to raise.

In fact, we commissioned a feasibility study to see if it was even possible for us to raise the amount ($5 million) we had calculated we would need to get started on this bigger goal. Our fundraising advisors interviewed a bunch of our donors, did their thing and came back with their report.

They had bad news. They told us it wasn't feasible. Our donor base was too narrow. Our organization was too young. In their professional opinion, they said we should expect to fall short of our goal.

But, they continued, something came out of our study that they had never seen before. For the first time ever, they heard donors say, "We don't think it will be possible for LifeWise to raise this much money, but we want them to try anyway. It's that important."

So we took their advice and launched our "First 1,000 Schools Campaign" with an initial fundraising goal of $5 million.

The full amount was pledged within nine months.

CENTURY CLUB (2022)

As I write this chapter, we are in the fall of 2022. I don't know yet if we'll make our big school goal by 2026. But I do know that things are looking pretty good.

When we worked out our year-by-year goals to reach 1,000 schools, the 2022 target was 84 total schools. That would keep us on track for 2026. How close did we get?

It's all in the Lord's hands, of course, and we're just happy to be along for the ride.

We're confirmed to serve more than 130 schools this school year.

And as I look at where we are and all that could be coming, it's hard not to be pretty excited. Because it looks to me like maybe that Death Star could be beginning to blow after all.

It's all in the Lord's hands, of course, and we're just happy to be along for the ride. We'll keep plugging away, trusting Him. But if it's His will, this whole thing could be exploding into a movement that none of us imagined possible.

FUNDING THE MISSION

Annual Fundraising Banquets *(Had to Take 2020 Off)*

2019

2021

2022

TRAINING THE TEAM

Annual Summit for Leaders

2020

2021

2022

RHONDA'S STORY

Scan to Watch Video

A LIFEWISE STORY
"Rhonda and Her $10 T-Shirt"

Rhonda is a director for a LifeWise program that launched in the fall of 2022.

After one late-night LifeWise event, she collapsed into bed. The next morning, still tired but needing to run some errands, she pulled on the same LifeWise t-shirt she'd worn the previous night and headed out, hoping NOT to be seen in her dirty shirt. No such luck.

All morning, her bright red LifeWise shirt acted more like a beacon as people she met stopped her to talk about LifeWise.

Lynda, the cashier at Marshalls, shared the wonderful things she'd heard about LifeWise. She said, "We have a broken world, but we must do something."

In the Kohls parking lot, someone yelled, "Go LifeWise!" It was a couple from a nearby town who raved about their LifeWise, and as they walked away, the husband said, "We need to wear our LifeWise shirts more often!"

Inside the store, her t-shirt reminded a retired school secretary that she wanted to sign up as a LifeWise

Each one saw her bright red shirt and wanted to share excitedly about their connection to LifeWise.

volunteer. A family friend saw her in Kohls, too; her granddaughters attended LifeWise. She was planning to volunteer, and her daughter was going to be a substitute teacher for the program. Rhonda even met a mom and two kids wearing LifeWise shirts, so she chatted about their town's plans to launch a LifeWise.

And it didn't stop there. At Hobby Lobby, the girl cutting fabric shared that her father's church was gathering signatures for a LifeWise. And in Meijer, an elderly gentleman stopped to ask about LifeWise. He'd seen something in the paper about it and wondered how they could launch a program in his town.

In a single morning, Rhonda had connected with friends and strangers from six local towns whose elementary schools included almost 3,000 students. Each one saw her bright red shirt and wanted to share excitedly about their connection to LifeWise.

By the time Rhonda finished her errands and headed home, she was absolutely in awe of the excitement for LifeWise in her area and even more thrilled to wear her LifeWise shirt every chance she got. It was almost as if a movement had started, a red-shirted tsunami of enthusiasm that was sweeping their schools.

And she was even more excited to be a part of it.

✦ ✨ ✦

CHAPTER 09

TIME FOR A MOVEMENT?
HOW LifeWise Looks Today

So far in this book, we've covered WHY we need to reinstall religious education during the public school day and HOW

to do it legally and effectively through released time (in general) and LifeWise Academy (specifically).

But is any of that really a movement? We don't know yet. But I can tell you, the ingredients are there.

THE MOVEMENT RECIPE

Of course, I'm the founder of LifeWise. So obviously I'm going to call what's going on a movement, right?

It's possible that I'm totally off base to think this way. It's possible that we're just patting ourselves on the back or have an inflated view of our own importance. It's possible.

But movements are real, in art or society or religious education. They can be defined. And according to those who know such things, every movement has three key ingredients:

1. It comes at the right time.
2. It forms because a new idea gains momentum.
3. And it always happens collectively—through a seemingly unstoppable group of sold-out people.[1]

We believe LifeWise is the start of a movement because all three of those ingredients are mixing and beginning to bake right now.

INGREDIENT #1: PERFECT TIMING

Sometimes we say that someone is in place "for such a time as this." The phrase was first used about a woman in the Bible (Esther), but the idea is that someone is showing up at just the right place at just the right time to accomplish something specific.

And I believe the same can be said of LifeWise. It has come to life at just the right moment.

By itself, it's just a program. But because it has arrived now, at exactly this moment, it is becoming more. So what is it about this time that is so perfect? A perfect storm of factors is falling into place. There are three big ones.

First, *right now* Christians are grasping the urgency of their mission.

In the face of major shifts in culture and the struggles schools are facing, many Christians are realizing we simply don't have time to waste. As Peter Kreeft put it, "When a maniac is at the door, feuding brothers reconcile."[2]

So these churches are coming together *for something* instead of just being *against* something else. They no longer want to be on the defensive. They have a mission. And LifeWise is the roadmap they are using to accomplish it.

Second, *right now* educators are recognizing the need for something unique, effective, and positive.

The amazing people doing the hard work of educating are tired. Every day, they face the overwhelming task of trying to do more with less. They must parent as well as teach. They are on the front lines of the negative mental health issues and various personal problems the students face, and they are acknowledging that they need something more. And LifeWise is providing the unique and positive support they desperately need.

Third, *right now* communities, especially parents, *want* to be involved again. It's not, of course, that they weren't interested before. And everyone knows family and community involvement is a key factor to a school's success (see chapter 3).

But right now, something is different. These communities are driven, in a new and exciting way, to actually get involved. They are stepping up big to see it happen. And they are using LifeWise Academy to get it done.

Urgency. Need. Involvement. This is a perfect storm. The timing could not be better.

INGREDIENT #2: POWERFULLY DIFFERENT

A movement is always based on an idea that is *different from* what has been the norm.

In a movement, the newness of the idea resonates. And it's not just different for the sake of being different. It feels real, true, engaging in a way that makes people connect with it deeply.

In the art world, this happened when impressionist painters suddenly refused to paint realistically. They used color, paint strokes and composition in new and powerful ways. It was shocking, but effective. And as people responded, the new style of painting exploded as a form all its own.

Of course, we aren't talking about art (thank goodness). But in education, it works the same way.

Released time has become the shocking "new" concept that people are connecting to and wanting to get involved with. LifeWise Academy is the tool that they are discovering. Our innovative approach is getting people's attention.

I have the honor of leading the charge, but the growing enthusiasm isn't based on me personally. In fact, not that long ago, I introduced myself to a local volunteer in a LifeWise shirt, and they had no idea who I was.

That's good. This movement we're seeing isn't about Joel Penton, the founder of LifeWise Academy.

It's not about a person. It's about a concept—a program that any community can use to bring the opportunity of released time into their schools and to their students. That's the idea people are connecting with and finding a new hope in. They want this (kind of old) new idea.

INGREDIENT #3: PEOPLE DRIVEN

LifeWise would have fizzled out quickly if it all depended on our staff team alone.

Instead, what we're seeing is a collective approach that is sweeping across schools and communities. In over a hundred schools (and counting), people have organized a program. Hundreds more communities are starting the same journey—together.

It's happening in wave after wave. And here's what it looks like.

A LIFEWISE
"Tidbit"

One of our programs was looking for a nearby location to hold LifeWise classes. Despite not having any personal connections there, they reached out to the Lutheran church across the street from the school. Would they be willing to host the LifeWise program? The church didn't even hesitate even though they hadn't run a children's ministry in over twenty years. They offered their entire basement to LifeWise, and now the sound of children's voices are regularly heard ringing through the church building again.

✦ ✧ ✦

Released time is inspiring churches and individual Christians to partner together.

It looks like unity.

The general perception of religion and religious folks tends to be one of fences, lines and separate spaces. For many reasons, that's not wrong. Nor is it always a bad thing.

Released time is inspiring churches and individual Christians to partner together in powerful ways, some for the first time ever.

I have been in community meetings with church leaders who have never worked together before. They have vastly different backgrounds and traditions. Methodists and Baptists and Lutherans are supporting the local school's LifeWise program *together*.

These partnerships are organic, not forced. Pastors are doing more than just "ministers' breakfasts" or a yearly community service. Through LifeWise Academy, they are linking arms in a real, practical way that has the potential for lasting, positive change in their communities. And they are thrilled.

These partnerships are also positive. Instead of spending time squabbling about nonessentials, local churches are working together to facilitate what is essential. Instead of just complaining about what they don't want to see, LifeWise is offering them a chance to work together toward a practical and positive solution to those problems.

We are seeing these partnerships everywhere, and they are the necessary foundation for any lasting movement.

It looks like sacrifice.

Movements are not easy. They require hard work, experience bad press and hit a lot of roadblocks as they roll. But when the people are committed, they also willingly sacrifice to see the movement succeed.

There have been major donations:

- ✦ To launch one particular LifeWise in northwest Ohio, we wanted to acquire a piece of land next to the school. It was owned by the mayor (his personal property, not the city's). So we scheduled a meeting with him. We looked at a map of the land, we told him about LifeWise, and at the end of the meeting, he asked what we wanted from him. I pointed at a plot of land on the map and said, "I'd like you to donate this land for a LifeWise program." So that's what he did.

- ✦ After a couple of rounds of LifeWise launches, it dawned on me that I should contact a particular superintendent from northwest Ohio whom I had met at a church years before. I emailed him to see if he had heard about LifeWise. He replied that he wanted to see a LifeWise started in his district and he'd be willing to donate $100,000 to make it happen.

- ✦ Someone else sent us *one million* dollars without even being asked. They had simply read through some of our literature and knew we needed funding. Seriously.

We've had people change careers to join the LifeWise movement:

- ✦ Our COO, Steve, transitioned from the private sector where he had been director of operations for a division of a Fortune 100 company so that he could help lead our little start-up ministry with operational excellence.

- ✦ One of our Program Directors, Kathryn, shut down her private law practice so she could focus on leading her local LifeWise team.

- ✦ Our Creative Director, Nathan, accepted a gig with LifeWise as his first "real job" after working as a freelance Emmy and Dove Award-winning filmmaker for more than a decade.

We've seen people willingly lend us their influence to spread the LifeWise story:

- Jim Tressel, the legendary Ohio State National Championship Coach (my coach), and his wife, Ellen, agreed to be honorary campaign chairs for our First 1,000 Schools campaign.
- The lieutenant governor of Ohio, Jon Husted, through the Ohio Office of Faith-Based Initiatives, has orchestrated meetings of community leaders around the state to introduce the concept of LifeWise.
- Many, many pastors have opened their Sunday morning services, giving their local LifeWise leaders the chance to share the LifeWise story with their congregations.

And we've had hundreds of everyday people—local directors, steering committee members and community and church members—give uncountable amounts of time and money to see LifeWise come alive in their communities.

These regular folks are making presentations even though they hate speaking in public. They're requesting donations even though no one likes talking about money. They are volunteering their time, land, expertise and skills to make LifeWise work. They are sacrificing. And they are seeing great rewards as a result.

MORE ON INGREDIENT #3

Ultimately, the third ingredient of a movement is the most important. It's all about people—God's people, in particular—coming together for a purpose larger than themselves.

And I'll let you in on a little secret—it's about more than any one program. I think LifeWise is great. But our purpose is to reinstall religious education into the public school day. Our goal is to reach kids with the gospel. Not to build a brand.

Which brings us to the final piece of the LifeWise puzzle. You. We need You.

So maybe someone doesn't like our plug and play model, and they want the adventure of starting a unique local program. Maybe someone doesn't like our color scheme or my speaking voice, and they decide to create their own scalable program like LifeWise that turns out to be even better. Whatever. Sounds awesome. Because it's not about us.

We're praying for a movement that is ultimately about seeing God do through His people what He always does—change lives.

When people are inspired to work together in such powerful ways, it changes them. And as more programs are started, more students and families are impacted positively. And as the lives of students are changed, even more people will be inspired to join the movement.

We are banking on exactly that. On God using our tiny program to provide the spark that changes the lives of countless students, families, communities, and churches.

But it starts with individuals. Which brings us to the final piece of the LifeWise puzzle.

You.

We need you.

BEV'S STORY

Scan to Watch Video

A LIFEWISE STORY
"The Bev Method"

Bev lives in a small town just west of Columbus that was starting the process to launch a LifeWise Academy. They began, as all LifeWise programs do, with Step One: building their Community Interest List. They needed at least fifty signatures.

One weekend, Bev sat down, intending to post on social media about LifeWise to build up interest and (hopefully) get more signatures for their list. In a moment of inspiration, however, she decided not to write a post. After all, she reasoned, the algorithm was likely to limit the reach of a simple post.

So instead, she began to scroll through her Facebook friends list.

In one weekend, their district's LifeWise Community Interest List grew by over a hundred names!

That Saturday, she sent a direct message to every one of her online contacts who lived in her school district, telling them about LifeWise and the opportunity they had to bring Bible education to local students during the school day.

In that one weekend, their district's LifeWise Community Interest List grew by over a hundred names!

Bev is not the director of her local LifeWise program. She's a mom with many other responsibilities. But today Bev's school district has a LifeWise program, in part because she simply and thoughtfully championed the effort in her community.

One private message at a time.

CHAPTER 10

THE LAST MISSING PIECE
HOW You Fit In

Do you know the single greatest hurdle LifeWise Academy faces?

It isn't separation of church and state or finances. It's not opposition from those who disagree with what we're trying to do. It's not even that we're figuring things out as we go.

It's actually much simpler than all of that. The single greatest hurdle we face is the knowledge gap—the reality that *nobody knows* about the amazing opportunity of released time.

Released time has been around for seventy years, but it hasn't penetrated more than a handful of schools and districts spread thinly across the country.

So if we want to see this LifeWise movement grow (which we do). And if we want to see it continue for decades (which we absolutely do), then what we need most of all is to get out the word about it.

People need to hear about LifeWise. Its benefits. Its possibilities. Its existence.

The very best way to spread this message is you. We need you to tell your LifeWise story.

THE POWER OF STORY

We've covered a lot of information and history in these pages, and I think it's all cool. That's why I wrote it all down, obviously.

But my favorite part of the book (and what my friends who read an earlier draft told me is their favorite part) is the LifeWise stories. They are the heart of the book. Because they are the heart of LifeWise.

All the dry, boring (but very important) stuff is necessary to explain the WHY and HOW of released time and of LifeWise. But when we tell the stories, everything changes.

When I sit with people and simply tell them the LifeWise story, more often than not they jump right in. Before I can even make a request, they ask, "How can I help?"

That's what we need you to do: help us share the LifeWise story by joining the movement and then telling others about your part in it.

What does that look like?

JOINING UP—CHECK THE STATUS OF YOUR LOCAL SCHOOL

Before you tell your story, you'll need to get familiar with the best tool for the job—your school district's Community Interest List webpage.

Every school district in the nation already has a page on our website. Every single one. So right now, go to *lifewise.org* and click "Find Your School" to check the status of your district.

If there is already an effort underway in your area, all the details you need to get connected will be there.

Most school districts don't have a launch effort underway yet. That's okay. That means you can be the first one to sign your local Community Interest List, which is actually pretty cool. Signing the list just means that you're saying, "Yes, I would like to see a LifeWise Academy started in my community."

So, go ahead. Find your school and sign your list.

Here's a QR code to take you directly to the page where you can search for your school. It's okay to take a break from reading. Just go there, sign up and come right back. I'll wait.

Did you do it? Did you sign your list?

Great. You now officially have a story to share about LifeWise. We'll call it "A LifeWise Story: The Day [Your Name] Read a Book, Caught the Vision and Signed the LifeWise Community Interest List."

It's a story I already want to read. And it's one others will want to hear too. Which brings us to the next step: start telling your story.

ELIMINATING ~~EXCUSES~~ RESERVATIONS

It sounds too simple, doesn't it?

That after you sign the Community Interest List, all we need you to do is start blabbing about LifeWise. Just telling the story. I can almost hear your concerns.

But, Joel, you might say, I don't know enough about LifeWise.

Sure you do. You've just read the book on it (literally). Yes, I might know a few more of the neat stories about LifeWise than you do, but if you've read these pages, then you know everything you need to know to get involved. And as you get involved, you'll have more of your own stories to tell.

But Joel, what if someone asks me something I don't know?

Okay, that's possible. Just say "I don't know." Then look for the info and get back to them. We've tried to make it incredibly easy to find information on LifeWise. We added a number of helpful appendices to this book. And the LifeWise website has a bunch of videos and information, stories and next steps you can watch and share.

But Joel, how do I even get started?

Like I said, it's as simple as telling someone your LifeWise story. You can even wear LifeWise gear (like Rhonda) and let the conversations roll.

But if you need a more detailed plan than just wearing cool merch, try our 20-20-20 rule. Send your Community Interest List link directly to 20 people through social media (be like Bev), 20 by email and 20 by text. No group messages. Send each one individually. Remember, you want to have a chance to tell the LifeWise story.

So just tell people about it? That's really it?

Yep, pretty much. We even have a cool team for you to join, if you want. It's called the LifeWise Street Team.

JOIN THE LIFEWISE STREET TEAM

Street Team members spread the word about LifeWise to build their local Community Interest List. Every community needs Street Team members. Register for the Street Team at ***lifewise.org/streetteam***, and you'll receive some extra resources to help you effectively spread the word.

Do Street Team members have to lead the LifeWise program?

Nope, they just spread the word. Our Street Team members are not always directors or steering committee members, though they absolutely can be.

And remember, the whole goal is to be you and tell your LifeWise story to spread the word in your community.

ONE FINAL WORD: THE REAL STORY

I get the privilege of telling my own LifeWise story a lot. I love to do it. I've seen God work throughout the journey in powerful ways, and it's a joy to share it with others.

But I also love to share others' stories just as much. Because it reminds me that God is really using LifeWise in the way we've been praying for—to change lives.

If this thing sweeps across the nation like we believe it can, we could see this story repeated millions of times over.

It changes the lives of people who support and lead LifeWise programs. You've met some of them in these pages: Tim and Vince and Julie and Rhonda. There are literally thousands of people just like them whose lives have been changed because of LifeWise.

Most importantly, though, it changes the lives of the students who attend LifeWise.

Remember Christian and his mom, Bethany, from page 72? Not long ago, I followed up to see how they were doing.

They are still attending church regularly. Christian is preparing to be baptized. And their family now personally donates to the local LifeWise program monthly so that more students can learn about God's love during school hours.

Bethany has even said of LifeWise, "Like our story, it might lead somebody to a church and change a whole household."

That's the real story. That's the opportunity of released time. That's the outcome LifeWise can have. And not just for Christian and his family.

If this thing sweeps across the nation like we believe it can, we could see this story repeated millions of times over. Maybe that sounds crazy. But if God decides to do it, I'd like to be along for the ride.

You can be, too. You can be part of changing lives all over this country. And all it takes is for you, like those you've met in this book, to tell your story.

So, are you in? Will you join the movement? Will you share your LifeWise story?

Fantastic. Let's get started.

4 WAYS TO GET INVOLVED

FIND YOUR LOCAL SCHOOL

Select Your State

SEARCH

lifewise.org/interest

Adams Central Community Schools

Alexandria Community School Corp

Anderson Community School Corp

Join the STREET TEAM

lifewise.org/streetteam

NO SKIPPING

Get LifeWise
SWAG

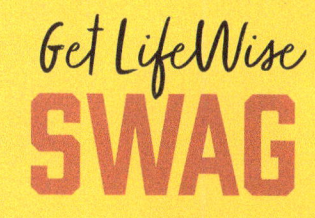

lifewise.org/store

lifewise.org/donate

Donate
TO REACH MORE STUDENTS

EXTR

You didn't know you needed to know!

A Things

Appendix 1: Nitty Gritty LifeWise FAQs
Appendix 2: Even More Impact
Acknowledgements
Endnotes
Bibliography

Appendix #1
NITTY GRITTY LIFEWISE FAQS

THE BIG PICTURE

Is teaching the Bible during the school day really legal?

Yes! The concept of released time religious instruction has been upheld multiple times at the U.S. Supreme Court. Released time guidelines both guard against government establishment of any one religion and allow expression of the right to the "free exercise of religion," also protected by the First Amendment.

Is LifeWise Academy a political movement?

No, LifeWise is not affiliated with or supportive of any particular political party or figure. LifeWise is for all families regardless of political persuasion.

Why should students, even those without a Christian background, learn about the Bible?

LifeWise Academy recognizes that the Bible was foundational to the forming of our society. We believe all students, regardless of religious background, can benefit from a greater understanding of such an influential book.

What's the history of LifeWise?

LifeWise Academy was founded in 2018 as a division of Stand For Truth, an event-based nonprofit ministry with a mission to reach public school students. The creation of LifeWise was inspired by a released time program in Van Wert, OH, which boasts a 95% participation rate among public elementary school students. Stand For Truth and the Van Wert released time program teamed up to create LifeWise Academy, launching the first two LifeWise programs in the fall of 2019. In September 2022, Stand For Truth was renamed as LifeWise, Inc. LifeWise Academy now serves more than five dozen school districts.

How does LifeWise compare with before- and after-school programs?

LifeWise is complementary to existing before- and after-school programs. The primary distinctive feature of LifeWise is that it operates during the school day, thereby engaging the students who are most unlikely to attend before- and after-school programs due to transportation, extracurricular and other issues.

How is LifeWise different from other released time programs?

LifeWise offers a structured, "plug and play" model which provides communities all the tools to launch and maintain an effective program while limiting administrative duties. The proven model also lends credibility to school administrators, parents, donors and volunteers.

CURRICULUM, SCHEDULE, AND CLASSROOM

Does LifeWise interfere with classes during the school day?

No, while classes are held during the school day, they do not interfere with children's mandatory courses or extracurricular activities. The class schedule is set by school personnel in consultation with LifeWise representatives. Usually, LifeWise classes are scheduled as part of the "specials" rotation or during times when other elective courses are offered.

What curriculum is taught?

The LifeWise curriculum is designed to take students through the entire Bible, beginning in Genesis and ending in Revelation, over the course of five years. Each lesson reviews a Bible passage as well as a "Living LifeWise" character trait. The lessons' order and activities are flexible and can be modified as the teacher finds necessary. Download a sample of the curriculum on our website.

How often are LifeWise classes?

Typically, students attend LifeWise once per week for a class lasting between 45 minutes and one hour.

How large are the class sizes?

LifeWise classes are usually the size of normal school classes, between 15 and 25 students.

Does LifeWise have protocols for behavioral issues?

Each LifeWise class should have two adult volunteers to aid teachers with behavioral issues as necessary. The default procedure for poor behavior is to escort the child back to the school through a process agreed upon by the LifeWise location and public school.

PERSONNEL

Who leads a local program?

A local Steering Committee first coordinates program details with school officials and then identifies a local Program Director and Board to lead the program long-term using resources and coaching from the LifeWise Support Center.

Who teaches the classes?

Local LifeWise leaders recruit and hire qualified teachers using the resources and coaching from the LifeWise Support Center.

What are the volunteer needs?

Volunteers are needed to walk the students to and from the school and assist in the classroom and help as needed.

CHURCH AND COMMUNITY

How do churches with differing beliefs and practices partner together to provide LifeWise to local students?

The LifeWise Statement of Faith, Philosophy of Ministry and Team Member Conduct are designed to focus on the core tenets of the Christian faith, particularly the gospel. A special effort is made to avoid teaching an official position on secondary issues.

Has there been local opposition to LifeWise?

The very rare and minimal opposition we've seen has been based on misconceptions, misunderstanding and false information regarding the legality of released time and LifeWise. The most effective strategy in dealing with local opposition is to direct people to ***lifewise.org*** and encourage them to explore the site and watch the video.

OPERATIONS

How can a parent elect to enroll their child in LifeWise?

Parents complete a LifeWise permission slip that is registered with the school office before their child may attend.

What happens if a parent wants to remove their child from LifeWise?

LifeWise is completely voluntary, and parents have the right to withdraw their child at any time for any reason.

How do students get to the off-site location?

Students either walk under the supervision of volunteer chaperones or are driven by bus or van to the off-site location.

How do you start a local LifeWise?

Communities collaborate with LifeWise staff on a three-phase launch process. Learn more about the process at ***lifewise.org/getstarted***.

What are the options for LifeWise classroom facilities?

A variety of solutions have been used for LifeWise facilities. Four primary types of released time facilities:

1. Existing Space – Rental or donated use of a church or other business
2. Renovation – Purchase existing property, like a home, and remodel as necessary
3. New Build – Construction using a LifeWise model design or unique local design
4. Modular – Using a LifeWise semi-permanent modular building or unique local design

If a local facility is built or renovated, who owns it?

Local real estate is always owned locally. If necessary, the LifeWise Support Center can help a local program with the process of creating a local nonprofit for the purposes of owning real estate.

Who assumes liability for students during LifeWise?

LifeWise assumes liability for students the moment they exit the school. LifeWise carries liability insurance and enforces extensive safety and security protocols.

Does each LifeWise Academy need its own insurance policy?

No, each local program is covered under the LifeWise, Inc. insurance policy paid for by the LifeWise Support Center.

> *NOTE: The cost of the following coverage for all local programs is paid by the LifeWise Support Center: Directors and Officers, Religious Freedom, Sexual Acts, Employment Practices, Property, Media Fallout, Medical Coverage, Income and Extra Expense and Donations. Building and Personal Property coverage, if applicable, is managed by the LifeWise Support Center, but the cost is passed along to the local program.*

Are background checks performed on all volunteers and teachers?

Yes, all local leaders, teachers and volunteers are required to complete a background screening to ensure the safety of the students and the program. Child safety video training is also provided.

Does each local LifeWise need to file for 501(c)(3) tax exempt status?

No, each local program has 501(c)(3) tax exempt status under the LifeWise umbrella.

Does each local program need its own name?

No, each program uses the name "LifeWise Academy" with a school district or geographical surname, whichever is most appropriate (e.g., "LifeWise River View").

FINANCES

How much does it cost to operate a local program?

The cost varies from location to location. Some of the most significant costs include:

1. Director/Teacher(s) – Local programs are encouraged, though not required, to hire a part-time paid Director and paid Teachers.

2. Facility/Transportation – These costs can vary greatly depending on whether a facility is donated, rented, purchased or built, and whether transportation to the off-site location is required.

3. Membership Fee – Curriculum, technological systems, liability insurance, background screenings, training, coaching, donation systems and receipting, etc. based on the number of students enrolled.

4. Miscellaneous – Classroom supplies, printing and postage for promotional materials, permission slips, thank you notes, initial launch and training fees ($3,000), endowment contributions, etc.

NOTE: Our numbers indicate a program can operate within the approximate cost range of $100–$300 per student per year depending mainly on local decisions regarding paid staff, facility and transportation.

How is LifeWise funded?

Each LifeWise program is funded by private donations through local fundraising efforts. There is no cost to schools or participating families.

How are the donations raised to support the program?

The LifeWise Support Center provides proven strategies, training and materials to local LifeWise leaders to effectively raise the necessary funds.

How do local programs receive donations?

Local programs can receive donations via check or online through their dedicated donation page at ***lifewise.org/donate***.

If a community raises funds to launch a local program and then decides not to proceed, what happens with the donations?

The donations will remain earmarked for the local area for one year from the date the launch is officially put on hold. If no additional donations for the local area are made after the one-year mark, funds raised will be redirected to the national launch fund. Additional donations will extend the one-year hold from the date of deposit.

Appendix #2
EVEN MORE IMPACT

I like to think of this appendix as Chapter 3: The Director's Cut.

You know how in movies like *The Lord of the Rings*, they make a four-hour film and then have to cut a bunch of stuff so people can watch it in the theaters in a reasonable amount of time. But then, when they release the DVD, they put all that cool stuff back so people can get all the details and extras they didn't even know they were missing.

That's what this appendix is—the cool stuff we would add into The Director's Cut.

Chapter 3 is a critical piece of this book. It's the proof that what we're promising to schools and students really can happen. But it's a lot. We knew it was a lot. And so we had to cut some stuff out.

Of course, we didn't cut it because it wasn't true or well proven. We just ran out of space. And we needed you not to get so bogged down you quit reading.

But because there's tons of information, sources, and proof that some crazy nerds out there would love to read, we created this extra resource. The same four areas, with extra research we had to cut but now get to put back in, plus some, new super-cool stuff to boot.

So if you have more questions or just want to read more in a particular area or just think (like I do) that all this proof is cool, it's all here for you in one place.

So dig in.

AREA OF IMPACT #1: CHARACTER EDUCATION

One education resource boils character down to "values, ethics, emotional maturity and a sense of civics."[1]

To put it simply, good character means having and living out good values. Because religion also focuses, at least to some extent, on good values, it has a unique ability to positively influence people's values.

One researcher put it this way: Religion may influence people "to avoid the vices (e.g., gluttony, lust, envy, pride) and practice the virtues (e.g., compassion, forgiveness, gratitude, hope)" that lead to a good and healthy life.[2]

General Character

When the Oakland released time program was reviewed, the National Council on Crime and Delinquency saw evidence that the students were developing good character. Students were learning to make wise choices and to apply that wisdom in practical ways.

They showed respect and manners. They were learning sound morals, such as "staying away from drugs/alcohol and treating others well, as well as many of the 10 Commandments."[3]

Honesty

As we saw in chapter 3, a student's religious background also increases a likelihood of honesty. In another study, business students were given "an opportunity to increase their chances of winning money by falsely reporting their performance on a word-search puzzle." The "strongest factor [to] predict honest reporting" was religiousness.[4]

Reduced Violent Behavior

There is a clear link, according to researchers, that violent behavior is reduced in the face of religion.

Simon Dein, a psychologist and anthropologist, noted, *"The literature is not disparate or contradictory* ... Religious measures are generally inversely related to deviance, and this is especially true among the most rigorous studies."[5]

Risk Behaviors - Drug and Alcohol Abuse

Weber & Pargament put it simply: "There is a negative relationship between religiousness and substance abuse."[6]

Koenig's analysis indicates the same. "Of the 86 studies that have examined levels of religiousness, 76 (88 percent) reported significantly less alcohol use/abuse among religious subjects," with 40 of those 76 studies focusing on teens and college students.[7]

And, he concludes simply, "Religiousness is also associated with less recreational drug use, again especially in younger persons."[8]

The National Longitudinal Study on Adolescent Health [also] ... concluded that when adolescents placed a high level of importance on prayer and religion, they also had high levels of self-esteem and low levels of alcohol and cigarette use.[9]

Risk Behaviors - Sexual Activity

Another significant area of risk behavior that concerns researchers is sexual activity.[10] But again, religion has a positive influence on this kind of behavior.

+ A 2009 study found that "the more religious a teenager, the later he or she began to engage in sexual intercourse [and] the longer the delay between first and second intercourse."[11]

+ Interestingly, a student's friends can strengthen the positive impact. "The more religious a teenager's friends, the stronger the delaying effect of his or her own religiousness on their sexual activity. Conversely, having less religious friends reduces the effect of the individual's religiousness."[12]

+ In study after study, researchers have found that "by far the strongest factors influencing not engaging in premarital sex at all are church attendance and the importance one places on religion."[13]

AREA OF IMPACT #2: MENTAL HEALTH

A significant amount of research has been done on the effect of religion on mental health and well-being. And the results are overwhelmingly positive. Here's a few more examples to illustrate the point.

Positive Mental Health

"Most studies have also found a positive association between religiosity and other factors associated with well-being such as optimism and hope ... self-esteem ... sense of meaning and purpose in life ... internal locus of control, [and] social support."[14]

According to Weber & Pargament, "Overall, this emerging research has demonstrated beneficial effects in the lives of the religious. Better mental health, greater well being, higher quality of life, and lower rates of depression, anxiety, and suicide have all been reported among more religious individuals."[15]

Koenig & Larson found that 79 of 100 studies "found religious beliefs and practices consistently related to greater life satisfaction, happiness, positive affect, and higher morale."[16] And that "religious beliefs and practices rooted within established religious traditions are generally associated with better mental health, higher social functioning, and fewer self-destructive tendencies."[17]

In another study, Koenig reports that "religious beliefs and practices are consistently related to greater life satisfaction, happiness, positive affect, morale, and other indicators of well being."[18]

Rachael Rettner summarizes the findings this way:

> A slew of research has tied being religious with better well-being and overall mental health. A number of studies have found that devout people have fewer symptoms of depression and anxiety, as well as a better ability to cope with stress. Certain religious practices may even change the brain in a way that boosts mental health, studies suggest.[19]

Religion as a Coping Mechanism

One of the most common findings among research studies is that religion is a positive influence on mental health primarily through the social support and coping skills that it provides.[20]

According to Dr. Harold G. Koenig, director of the Center for Spirituality, Theology and Health at Duke University Medical Center, "People who are more involved in religious practices and who are more religiously committed seem to cope better with stress," Koenig said. "One of the reasons is because [religion] gives people a sense of purpose and meaning in life, and that helps them to make sense of negative things that happen to them."[21]

And Weber & Pargament note, "Positive religious coping methods (e.g., spiritual support, positive religious reframing of stressors, and spiritual connectedness) are significantly associated with and predictive of better mental health and psychological well being generally. Specifically, positive religious coping correlates with reductions in depression and anxiety."[22]

Decreased Rates of Suicide/Anxiety/Depression

This link is especially clear, so I will simply list some more of the research here:

- "In general, adolescents who have higher levels of spirituality and religiosity fare better than their less religious or spiritual peers—they have lower rates of risky health behaviors and fewer mental health problems and utilize spiritual coping to manage physical illness—even when controlling for other relevant demographic variables."—from a study published in the Journal of Adolescent Health.[23]

- Studies on "major cities ... reported powerful religious effects: the higher the church membership rate of an [area], the lower its suicide rate ... even when other factors such as rapid population turnover are taken into account."[24]

- "Wright and co-authors [14] found that spirituality, defined as the importance of religion in understanding one's meaning of life, and the role of religious beliefs in one's interactions in life, were directly associated with lower levels of depressive symptoms in adolescents (p .05)."[25]

- A 2015 review examining over 3000 scholarly articles ... found a "positive effect" of religion/spirituality on a variety of health outcomes, including: "minor depression, faster recovery from depressive episodes, lower rates of suicide, less use, abuse, and substance dependence, greater well-being, and self-reported happiness."[26]

- "People who report a closer connection to God experience a number of health-related benefits: less depression and higher self-esteem (Maton, 1989b), less loneliness (Kirkpatrick, Kellas, & Shillito, 1993), greater relational maturity (Hall & Edwards, 1996, 2002), and greater psychosocial competence (Pargament et al., 1988)."[27]

> ✦ "We located 101 studies that examined the relationship between religion and depression ... Again the majority found lower depression among the more religious."[28]

Stark sums it up for us nicely:

> Why does religiousness produce these psychological benefits? ... the larger part probably reflects the capacity of religion to offer people hope and purpose, and to comfort them in the face of life's disappointments and tragedies.[29]

AREA OF IMPACT #3: ACADEMIC ACHIEVEMENT

There is a surprisingly strong case for the positive influence of religion on academic achievement. But there is more we can add to the conversation.

General Achievement

A study of "rural Iowa families [found] that religiously involved youth tend to excel in school, and as their religiosity increased, so did their academic progress."[30]

There is also positive impact on long-term academic outcomes, such as graduation rates and college enrollment. "The more often students attended church, the more likely they were to enroll in college," Stark noted.[31]

"Dai found that more religiously involved students were ... more likely to aspire to attend four-year colleges and graduate school than were less involved students."[32]

And Barret reports that "religious socialization ... relates positively to a range of educational outcomes, including heightened educational expectations and increased standardized test scores."[33]

Won't Released Time Harm Struggling Students?

Some have expressed concerns that released time, in particular, will do more harm than good by removing struggling students from instruction time in the regular classroom. The result, they suggest, will be lower test scores.

This has not proven to be the case, however. Religious education, in particular, has shown no negative effects on test scores.

Students in the Oakland released time program performed as well as, or better than, their non-participating classmates on various literacy components such as comprehension.[34]

And "Latino students who took part in released time" showed no "significant difference" from "their matched peers on English and math test scores."[35]

At-Risk Advantage

The connection between religion and education has been a common theme of research, especially for at-risk students.

Mark Regnerus concludes that, "as the level of poverty rises within the neighborhood, the relationship between church attendance and being on-track in school becomes more positive, indicating a uniquely protective influence of church attendance among youth in more impoverished neighborhoods."[36]

In fact, he says, "Church attendance indeed strengthens the educational progress among children in high-poverty neighborhoods, regardless of how the latter is measured."[37]

The Achievement Gap

There is little doubt that a major achievement gap does exist between various groups of American students, most specifically between white and Black students. While some progress has been made in some areas, there is a connection between religion and reducing the achievement gap.

Rodney Stark notes that this gap is "considerably smaller in religious schools than in the public schools." It is also small "among students who are religious." It is also smaller when students live with both their father and mother. He continues:

> When William Jeynes combined all three factors, he found that among religious students at religious schools, and among students who come from intact families, there is no academic achievement gap. Under those conditions, African American students do as well as whites, and both groups excel.[38]

Jeyes concluded that schools should do more to "[incorporate] the strength that factors beyond the school confines can provide. The results of this study suggest that the religious faith of students may be such a source of strength."[39] Along those lines, then, allowing for religious education during the public school day may provide one such source of strength for students to build from.

AREA OF IMPACT #4: COMMUNITY INVOLVEMENT

Schools with high levels of community and family involvement, and especially religious community and family involvement, generally see students excel in both academic and extracurricular paths and achieve greater academic outcomes than those without.

But even more interesting is the concept of moral communities.

Moral Communities

Rodney Stark describes a moral community as a group or region where religious values and standards "inform" what people do. If a small number of people in the community are religious, their effect is muffled inside the greater non-religious context. Where religious people are the majority, religion begins to affect even the non-religious group.

This is relevant here because, as Stark notes, "Mark Regnerus of the University of Texas found that high schools can function effectively as moral communities and that the effect is not simply on/off but a matter of degree."[40]

In other words, as a school's students are more informed by religious values and ideals, the overall community begins to benefit from the religious effect. This possibility has great promise as (we hope) released time continues to spread to schools across the nation.

Each individual building can benefit from the influence of the religious education of the students who choose to participate.

FINAL THOUGHTS

So that's the Director's Cut. I hope you enjoyed the extra detail and new additions it provides. But even still, I've only given you the tip of the iceberg here.

Every day, more research is published that further traces the connection between religion and education. And from what we can see, the connection is powerful and positive in almost every way.

ACKNOWLEDGEMENTS

LifeWise runs on sacrifice.

We are not a business selling widgets. We are a movement, taking the love of God to those who need it. Every inch of progress we've made has come as the result of someone making a sacrifice.

Words cannot express my gratitude for all those who have sacrificed for this book and all that it represents. A short list of those heroes is below.

- **My Wife** - Bethany, you didn't fully know what you were signing up for 18 years ago when you married me. The Lord was kind to bless me with you.

- **My Children** - Joel III, Judah, Luther, Vera and Levi, you share me a lot. Sometimes too much. Thank you for your grace!

- **My Parents** - Whether driving to middle school wrestling matches, OSU football games or LifeWise banquets, no one cheers louder.

- **My Church** - Pastor Harrell and the NWB Family, we know we are so loved, so supported, so challenged to keep going!

- **Our Board** - It's easy to be bold when you're holding the rope.
- **Our Staff** - It takes a special person to sign on to this team. The Lord is using you!
- **Our Volunteers** - To the walkers, bus drivers, prayer warriors and everyone else giving your time, you are the hands and feet of our Lord!
- **Our Donors** - We are humbled. Your trust means so much! Look at what God is doing through your generosity!
- **The Editor** - Shannah, as always, you've done a magnificent job at a nearly impossible task—making sense out of my thoughts.
- **The Review Team** - The fingerprints of your feedback are all over this book. Thank you!
- **The One True King** - We have freely received grace from You. What joy it is to give of ourselves to honor You and impact others!

ENDNOTES

CHAPTER 1

1. "Common School Movement," Education Encyclopedia, 2022, accessed November 20, 2022, https://education.stateuniversity.com/pages/1871/Common-School-Movement.html.

2. E. Jennifer Monaghan, "Literacy Instruction and Gender in Colonial New England," *American Quarterly* 40, no. 1 (March 1988): 30, accessed November 23, 2022, https://www.jstor.org/stable/2713140.

3. Monaghan, 20–21.

4. Clarence H. Benson, *A Popular History of Christian Education* (Chicago: Moody, 1943), 109.

5. David Carleton, "Old Deluder Satan Act of 1647," *First Amendment Encyclopedia*, 2009, accessed November 11, 2022, https://www.mtsu.edu/first-amendment/article/1032/old-deluder-satan-act-of-1647.

6. "Common School Movement."

7. Benson, 140.

8. "BLS History," Boston Latin School, accessed April 22, 2022, https://www.bls.org/apps/pages/index.jsp?uREC_ID=206116&type=d.

9. "Common School Movement."

10. Benson, 114.

11. David Carleton, "Horace Mann," *The First Amendment Encyclopedia*, 2009, accessed November 30, 2022. https://mtsu.edu/first-amendment/article/1283/horace-mann.

12. "William Holmes McGuffey and His Readers," *The Museum Gazette*, National Park Service, January 1993, accessed December 7, 2022, http://www.countryschoolassociation.org/uploads/1/0/0/3/100377070/npsmcguffey__1_.pdf.

13. Robert Marquand, "The Rise and Fall of the Bible in US Classrooms," *Christian Science Monitor*, September 5, 1985, accessed April 24, 2022, https://www.csmonitor.com/1985/0905/dback3-f.html#.

14. "William Holmes McGuffey and His Readers."

15. Ibid.

16. Ibid.

17. "Common School Movement."

18. Deeptha V. Thattai, "A History of Public Education in the United States Editorial Summary," *ResearchGate* (2017), https://www.researchgate.net/publication/321179948.

19. Michael B. Katz, "The Origins of Public Education: A Reassessment," *History of Education Quarterly* 16, no. 4 (Winter 1976): 383–84, http://www.jstor.org/stable/367722.

20. David Masci, "Darwin and His Theory of Evolution," February 4, 2009, accessed May 11, 2022, https://www.pewresearch.org/religion/2009/02/04/darwin-and-his-theory-of-evolution/.

21. Lee Strobel, *The Case for Faith* (Grand Rapids, MI: Zondervan, 2000), 89.

22. David Hildebrand, "John Dewey," *The Stanford Encyclopedia of Philosophy*, Edward N. Zalta, ed, Winter 2021, accessed May 11, 2022, https://plato.stanford.edu/archives/win2021/entries/dewey/.

23. *Marquand*, "Rise and Fall."

24. Jeff Myers, *Truth Changes Everything* (Grand Rapids: Baker Books, 2022), 105.

25. *Marquand*, "Rise and Fall."

26. Artemus Ward, "Everson v. Board of Education (1947)," *First Amendment Encyclopedia*, 2009, accessed October 21, 2022, https://mtsu.edu/first-amendment/article/435/everson-v-board-of-education.

27. David L. Hudson, Jr. "Engel v. Vitale (1962)," *First Amendment Encyclopedia*, 2009, accessed June 7, 2022, https://www.mtsu.edu/first-amendment/article/665/engel-v-vitale.

28. John R. Vile, "Abington School District v. Schempp (1963)," *First Amendment Encyclopedia*, 2009, accessed June 7, 2022, https://www.mtsu.edu/first-amendment/article/1/abington-school-district-v-schempp.

CHAPTER 2

1. Jill Barshay, Hillary Flynn, Chelsea Sheasley, Talia Richman, Dahlia Bazzaz, and Rebecca Griesbach, "America's Reading Problem: Scores Were Dropping Even before the Pandemic." *The Hechinger Report*, November 10, 2021, accessed December 20, 2022, https://hechingerreport.org/americas-reading-problem-scores-were-dropping-even-before-the-pandemic.

2. Jill Barshay, "Proof Points: Why Reading Comprehension Is Deteriorating," *The Hechinger Report*, May 17, 2021, accessed December 20, 2022, https://hechingerreport.org/proof-points-why-reading-comprehension-is-deteriorating/; "Fast Facts: Reading," NCES, 2022, accessed December 20, 2022, https://nces.ed.gov/fastfacts/display.asp?id=147; "NAEP Report Card: 2022 NAEP Reading Assessment," NAEP, 2022, accessed December 20, 2022, https://www.nationsreportcard.gov/highlights/reading/2022/.

3. "ACT Test Scores in US Fall to Lowest in 30 Years," *VOA News*, October 15, 2022, accessed December 20, 2022, https://learningenglish.voanews.com/a/act-test-scores-in-us-fall-to-lowest-in-30-years/6788531.html; Jessica Logan, et. al., "Has Ohio's Third-Grade Reading Guarantee Led to Reading Improvements?" The Ohio State University CCEC, Spring 2019, accessed December 20, 2022, https://crane.osu.edu/files/2020/01/Third-Grade-Reading-Whitepaper_032019_WEB2-1.pdf; Lisa M. Treleaven, "Quantitative Insights into the Academic Outcomes of Homeschools from the Classic Learning Test," *Home School Researcher*, 38, no. 1 (2022): 1–13, accessed December 20, 2022, https://www.nheri.org/wp-content/uploads/2022/12/HSR381-Treleaven-article-only.pdf.

4. "Fast Facts: Long-term Trends in Reading and Mathematics Achievement," NCES, 2022, accessed December 20, 2022, https://nces.ed.gov/fastfacts/display.asp?id=38; "Fast Facts: Mathematics," NCES, 2022, accessed December 20, 2022, https://nces.ed.gov/fastfacts/display.asp?id=514; "NAEP Report Card: 2022 NAEP Mathematics Assessment," NAEP, 2022, accessed December 20, 2022, https://www.nationsreportcard.gov/highlights/mathematics/2022/.

5. Drew Desilver, "U.S. Students' Academic Achievement Still Lags That of Their Peers in Many Other Countries," Pew Research Center, February 15, 2017, accessed December 20, 2022, https://www.pewresearch.org/fact-tank/2017/02/15/u-s-students-internationally-math-science/; Maria Stephens, et. al, "Changes Between 2011 and 2019 in Achievement Gaps Between High- and Low-Performing Students in Mathematics and Science: International Results From TIMSS," IES, October 2022, accessed December 20, 2022, https://nces.ed.gov/pubs2022/2022041.pdf.

6. Rodney Stark, *America's Blessings: How Religion Benefits Everyone, Including Atheists* (Conshohocken, PA: Templeton Press, 2012), 137–139; William H. Jeynes, "Religiosity, Religious Schools, and Their Relationship with the Achievement Gap: A Research Synthesis and Meta-Analysis," *The Journal of Negro Education* 79, no. 3 (2010): 263–79. Accessed May 14, 2020, www.jstor.org/stable/20798348; Alan Vanneman, Linda Hamilton, and Janet Baldwin Anderson, "Achievement Gaps: How Black and White Students in Public Schools Perform in Mathematics and Reading on the National Assessment of Educational Progress," U.S. Dept. of Education, July 2009, accessed December 20, 2022, https://nces.ed.gov/nationsreportcard/pdf/studies/2009455.pdf.

7. Felicia Bolden, "Narrowing Achievement Gaps for At-Risk Students," Educator's Blog, February 13, 2020, accessed December 20, 2022, https://www.graduateprogram.org/2020/02/narrowing-achievement-gaps-for-at-risk-students/; Jianping Shen, Xuejin Lu, and Joseph Kretovics, "Improving the Education of Students Placed at Risk Through School-University Partnerships," *Educational Horizons* 82, no. 3 (2004): 184–193, https://www.jstor.org/stable/42926499.

8. Julia Lara and Kenneth Noble, "Chronic Absenteeism," NEA Research Brief 57 (2018), accessed November 2, 2022, https://files.eric.ed.gov/fulltext/ED595241.pdf; Arielle Mitropoulos, "Thousands of Students Reported 'Missing' from Schools Systems Nationwide amid Covid-19 Pandemic," ABC News, March 2, 2021, accessed October 18, 2022, https://abcnews.go.com/US/thousands-students-reported-missing-school-systems-nationwide-amid/story?id=76063922; Steven B. Sheldon and Joyce L. Epstein, "Getting Students to School: Using Family and Community Involvement to Reduce Chronic Absenteeism," *School Community Journal* 14, no. 2 (2004): 39–56, accessed May 31, 2022, https://files.eric.ed.gov/fulltext/EJ794822.pdf.

9. "Fast Facts: School Crime," NCES, 2022, accessed December 20, 2022, https://nces.ed.gov/fastfacts/display.asp?id=49; "Youth Risk Behavior Survey: Data Summary & Trends Report 2009–2019," CDC, 2019, www.cdc.gov/healthyyouth.

10. N. F. Kahn and R. Graham, eds., "The Current Landscape of Adolescent Risk Behavior," In *Promoting Positive Adolescent Health Behaviors and Outcomes: Thriving in the 21st Century* (Washington, DC: National Academies Press, 2019), https://www.ncbi.nlm.nih.gov/books/NBK554988/; "Youth Risk Behavior Survey: Data Summary & Trends Report 2009–2019," CDC, 2019, www.cdc.gov/healthyyouth.

11. "Bullying and Cyberbullying," SchoolSafety.gov, 2022, accessed December 20, 2022, https://www.schoolsafety.gov/bullying-and-cyberbullying?subtopic%5B107%5D=107#-block-views-block-resources-by-subtopic-block-1; "Facts About Bullying," StopBullying.gov, September 9, 2021, accessed December 20, 2022, https://www.stopbullying.gov/resources/facts; "Fast Facts: Bullying," NCES, 2022, accessed December 20, 2022, https://nces.ed.gov/fastfacts/display.asp?id=719.

12. "Bullying and Cyberbullying," SchoolSafety.gov, 2022, accessed December 20, 2022, https://www.schoolsafety.gov/bullying-and-cyberbullying?subtopic%5B107%5D=107#-block-views-block-resources-by-subtopic-block-1; "How Students Can Benefit from Character Education," Teachnology.com, accessed May 26, 2022, https://www.teach-nology.com/current-trends/character_education/.

13. Culture Translator. "Mr. Beast's Burgers, Rings of Sour, and Spoonies." Axis.org email, https://app.axis.org/explore/ctp-2022-09-09.

14. William Brangham and Gretchen Frazee, "Growing Number of Young Americans Feel Climate Anxiety," PBS NewsHour, November 10, 2021, accessed December 20, 2022, https://www.pbs.org/newshour/show/growing-number-of-young-americans-feel-climate-anxiety-heres-what-they-need-to-cope; "Data and Statistics on Children's Mental Health," CDC, June 3, 2022, accessed December 20, 2022, https://www.cdc.gov/childrensmentalhealth/data.html; "Mental Health," CDC, September 12, 2022, accessed December 20, 2022, https://www.cdc.gov/healthyyouth/mental-health/index.htm. "More than 1 in 3 high school students had experienced persistent feelings of sadness or hopelessness in 2019, a 40 percent increase since 2009."

15. "Mental Health," CDC, September 12, 2022, accessed December 20, 2022, https://www.cdc.gov/healthyyouth/mental-health/index.htm. "In 2019, approximately 1 in 6 youth reported making a suicide plan in the past year, a 44% increase since 2009."

16. "The Whole Child Approach to Education," ASCD, 2015, accessed August 31, 2022, http://www.wholechildeducation.org/about/.

17. Paul Barnwell, "Students' Broken Moral Compasses," *The Atlantic*, July 25, 2016, accessed December 30, 2022, https://www.theatlantic.com/education/archive/2016/07/students-broken-moral-compasses/492866/. "William Anderson, a high-school teacher in Denver, … emphasized that schools should promote this approach [blending academics "with an exploration of character and ethics"] to develop well-rounded students. Addressing academic skills and challenging students to consider ethics and character should not, he argued, be mutually exclusive."

18. Jeff Myers, *Unquestioned Answers: Rethinking Ten Christian Cliches to Rediscover Biblical Truths* (Colorado Springs, CO: David C Cook, 2020), 120–21.

19. Max Glaskin, "The Science Behind Spokes," Cyclist UK, April 28, 2015, accessed October 13, 2022, https://www.cyclist.co.uk/in-depth/85/the-science-behind-spokes.

20. C.S. Lewis, *Mere Christianity* (New York: Book-of-the-Month Club, 1997), 9–10.

21. Steven Spielberg, director, *Jurassic Park*, 1993, Universal, 1993, 127 min.

CHAPTER 3

1. My answer, in case you were wondering, was that he needed to wait for the community to bring a proposal and that he could cooperate with the effort but not explicitly encourage or discourage participation.

2. Erkan Acar, "Effects of Social Capital on Academic Success: A Narrative Synthesis," *Educational Research and Reviews* 6, no. 6 (June 2011): 456–461, accessed May 26, 2022, http://www.academicjournals.org/ERR; Sunia Fukofuka, "The Impact of Spirituality on Academic Performance," *International Forum* 10, no. 2 (October 2007), 37, accessed May 21, 2022, https://scholar.

google.com.ph/citations?view_op=view_citation&hl=en&user=0Os8InUAAAAJ&citation_for_view=0Os8InUAAAAJ:u5HHmVD_uO8C; William H. Jeynes, "Religiosity, Religious Schools, and Their Relationship with the Achievement Gap: A Research Synthesis and Meta-Analysis," The Journal of Negro Education 79, no. 3 (2010): 263–79. www.jstor.org/stable/20798348; William H. Jeynes, "The Effects of Religious Commitment on the Academic Achievement of Black and Hispanic Children," Urban Education 34, no. 4 (1999): 458–479. http://citeseerx.ist.psu.edu/viewdoc/download?doi=10.1.1.860.6145&rep=rep1&type=pdf.

3. Thomas Lickona, "Character Education: The Heart of School Reform," *Religion & Education* 27, no. 1 (2000): 59, https://doi.org/10.1080/15507394.2000.11000917.

4. "How Students Can Benefit from Character Education," Teachnology.com, accessed May 26, 2022, https://www.teach-nology.com/currenttrends/character_education/.

5. Jessica Spallino, "How Character Education Helps Kids Learn and Develop," Method Schools, January 23, 2017, accessed October 23, 2022, https://www.methodschools.org/blog/how-character-education-helps-kids-learn-and-develop.

6. Gary Skaggs and Nancy Bodenhorn, "Relationships between Implementing Character Education, Student Behavior, and Student Achievement," *Journal of Advanced Academics* 18, no. 1 (2006): 107, https://files.eric.ed.gov/fulltext/EJ753972.pdf.

7. Monique W. Morris, Barry Krisberg, and Sharan Dhanoa, "Summary of Findings: Released Time Bible Education," National Council on Crime and Delinquency (2003): 11, accessed May 2020, https://california.foundationcenter.org/reports/summary-of-findings-released-time-bible-education/.

8. Rodney Stark, *America's Blessings: How Religion Benefits Everyone, Including Atheists* (Conshohocken, PA: Templeton Press, 2012), 53.

9. Christopher A. Was, Dan J. Woltz, and Clif Drew, "Evaluating Character Education Programs and Missing the Target: A Critique of Existing Research," *Educational Science Review* 1 (2006): 148–156, doi:10.1016/j.edurev.2006.08.001.

10. Stark, 55.

11. Ibid, 4–5.

12. Brian Barrett, "Religion and Habitus: Exploring the Relationship between Religious Involvement and Educational Outcomes and Orientations among Urban African American Students," *Urban Education* 45, no. 4 (2010): 464, accessed March 22, 2022, DOI: 10.1177/0042085910372349.

13. Mark D. Regnerus, "Making the Grade: The Influence of Religion upon the Academic Performance of Youth in Disadvantaged Communities," Baylor ISR: Baylor University, 2008, accessed May 21, 2022, 11, http://www.baylorisr.org/wp-content/uploads/ISR_Making_Grade.pdf.

14. Stark, 37.

15. Harold G. Koenig and David B. Larson, "Religion and Mental Health: Evidence for an Association," *International Review of Psychiatry* 13, no. 2 (2001): 75.

16. Simon Dein, Christopher CH Cook, and Harold Koenig, "Religion, Spirituality, and Mental Health: Current Controversies and Future Directions," *The Journal of Nervous and Mental Disease* 200, no. 10 (2012): 5.

17. Koenig and Larson, 71.

18. Meg Anderson and Kavitha Cardoza, "Mental Health in Schools: A Hidden Crisis Affecting Millions of Students," nprED, August 31, 2016, https://www.npr.org/sections/

ed/2016/08/31/464727159/mental-health-in-schools-a-hidden-crisis-affecting- millions-of-students.

19. Koenig and Larson, 71.

20. Samuel R. Weber and Kenneth I. Pargament, "The Role of Religion and Spirituality in Mental Health," *Current Opinion in Psychiatry* 27, no. 5 (2014): 358–363.

21. Stark, 107–08.

22. Stark, 95.

23. Koenig and Larson, 71.

24. Maria Archer, "The Positive Effects of Religion on Mental Illness." Institute for Family Studies, July 28, 2017, https://ifstudies.org/blog/the-positive-effects-of-religion-on-mental-illness. Citing Koenig, 289.

25. Sunia Fukofuka, "The Impact of Spirituality on Academic Performance." *International Forum* 10, no. 2 (October 2007), 37, accessed May 21, 2022, https://scholar.google.com.ph/citations?view_op=view_citation&hl=en&user=0Os8InUAAAAJ&citation_for_view=0Os8InUAAAAJ:u5HHmVD_uO8C.

26. Regnerus, "Making the Grade," 6.

27. Fukofuka, 36.

28. Ibid.

29. Stark, 134.

30. Ibid.

31. qtd. in Stark, 135.

32. [text box] Christian Smith, qtd. in Stark, 135.

33. [text box] Mark Regnerus, Christian Smith, and Melissa Fritsch, "Religion in the Lives of American Adolescents: A Review of the Literature," *A Research Report of the National Study of Youth and Religion* No. 3. Chapel Hill, NC: UNC, 2003, 14, accessed May 21, 2022, https://files.eric.ed.gov/fulltext/ED473896.pdf.

34. [text box] Ilana M. Horwitz, Benjamin W. Domingue, and Kathleen Mullan Harris, "Not a Family Matter: The Effects of Religiosity on Academic Outcomes Based on Evidence from Siblings," *Social Science Research* (2020): 88–89, accessed May 27, 2022, https://doi.org/10.1016/j.ssresearch.2020.102426.

35. Regnerus, "Making the Grade," 8.

36. Ivory A. Toldson and Kenneth Alonzo Anderson, "Editor's Comment: The Role of Religion in Promoting Academic Success for Black Students," *The Journal of Negro Education* 79, no. 3 (2010), 206, accessed May 19, 2020, www.jstor.org/stable/20798343.

37. Regnerus, Smith, and Fritsch, 18.

38. Regnerus, "Making the Grade," 5.

39. Stark, 137.

40. Patrick F. Fagan, "Religious Practice and Educational Attainment," *MarriResearch* (2010), 22, https://downloads.frc.org/EF/EF12D59.pdf.

41. David R. Hodge, "Latino Students and Spiritual Release Time Programs: Does Releasing

Students from Class for Spiritual Instruction Impede Academic Achievement?" *Families in Society: The Journal of Contemporary Social Services* 93, no. 2 (2012): 146.

42. J. Luke Wood and Adriel A Hilton, "Spirituality and Academic Success: Perceptions of African American Males in the Community College," (2012), 44, https://works.bepress.com/jluke_wood/12/; William H. Jeynes, "The Effects of Religious Commitment on the Academic Achievement of Black and Hispanic Children," *Urban Education* 34, no. 4 (1999): 473, http://citeseerx.ist.psu.edu/viewdoc/download?doi=10.1.1.860.6145&rep=rep1&type=pdf.

43. William H. Jeynes, "Religiosity, Religious Schools, and Their Relationship with the Achievement Gap: A Research Synthesis and Meta-Analysis," *The Journal of Negro Education* 79, no. 3 (2010): 273, www.jstor.org/stable/20798348.

44. Ibid, 275.

45. "Parent, Family, Community Involvement in Education," NEA Policy Brief, 2008, https://www.coursehero.com/file/35617307/NEA-Poliy-Brief-Parent-Family-Community-Involvment-pdf/.

46. Barrett, 449.

47. Barrett, 457.

48. Regnerus, "Making the Grade," 11.

49. Barrett, 457.

50. Regnerus, "Making the Grade," 5.

51. "Parent, Family, Community Involvement in Education."

CHAPTER 4

1. *Marquand*, "Rise and Fall."

2. John R. Vile, "Board of Education of the City of Cincinnati v. Minor (1872)," *First Amendment Encyclopedia*, 2009, accessed May 11, 2022, https://www.mtsu.edu/first-amendment/article/660/board-of-education-of-the-city-of-cincinnati-v-minor.

3. Skaggs, 84.

4. Barnwell, "Students' Broken Moral Compass." "By omission, are U.S. schools teaching their students that character, morality, and ethics aren't important in becoming productive, successful citizens?"

5. William H. Jeynes, "A Meta-Analysis on the Relationship Between Prayer and Student Outcomes," *Education and Urban Society* 52, no. 8 (2020), 1232.

6. Ibid, 1232, emphasis added.

7. Ibid, 1232.

8. Jude Schwalbach, "Combating Value-Neutrality and Creating Classrooms of Character," *The Heritage Foundation*, December 13, 2019, accessed December 30, 2022, https://www.heritage.org/education/commentary/combating-value-neutrality-and-creating-classrooms-character.

9. Ibid.

10. Liraz Margalit, "The Psychology of Choice," *Psychology Today* October 3, 2014, accessed November 20, 2022, https://www.psychologytoday.com/us/blog/behind-online-behavior/201410/the-psychology-choice.

11. "Christian Parents Want Education Quality and Their Values Too, According to New

Stride, Inc. Survey," Business Wire, August 3, 2022, accessed October 17, 2022, https://www.businesswire.com/news/home/20220803005183/en/Christian-Parents-Want-Education-Quality-and-Their-Values-Too-According-to-New-Stride-Inc.-Survey; Sarah Grady, "A Fresh Look at Homeschooling in the U.S.," NCES Blog, Sept. 26, 2017, accessed July 10, 2020, https://nces.ed.gov/blogs/nces/post/a-fresh-look-at-homeschooling-in-the-u-s; "Private School FAQs," Council for American Private Education, 2020, accessed July 10, 2020, https://www.capenet.org/facts.html.

12. Ryan Foley, "63% of Americans Think Parents Should Have 'Final Say' in Education," *The Christian Post*, November 20, 2021, accessed October 18, 2022, https://www.christianpost.com/news/parents-should-have-final-say-in-public-education-survey.html; Jude Schwalbach, "Combating Value Neutrality." "As University of Arkansas professor Jay Greene explains, educational endeavors that focus on local communities succeed, where attempts to reform mammoth school systems through heavy-handed top-down government approaches have repeatedly failed."

CHAPTER 5

1. Hana M. Ryman and J. Mark Alcorn, "Establishment Clause (Separation of Church and State)," *First Amendment Encyclopedia*, 2009, accessed June 7, 2022, https://www.mtsu.edu/first-amendment/article/885/establishment-clause-separation-of-church-and-state.

2. John M. Barry, "God, Government, and Roger Williams' Big Idea," *Smithsonian Magazine*, January 2012, accessed June 7, 2022, https://www.smithsonianmag.com/history/god-government-and-roger-williams-big-idea-6291280/.

3. John S. Baker, Jr, "Wall of Separation," *First Amendment Encyclopedia*. 2009, accessed June 7, 2022, https://www.mtsu.edu/first-amendment/article/886/wall-of-separation.

4. [text box] Barry, "God, Government, and Roger Williams' Big Idea."

5. [text box] Matthew Harris, "Virginia Statute for Religious Freedom," *First Amendment Encyclopedia*, 2009, accessed June 7, 2022, https://mtsu.edu/first-amendment/article/880/virginia-statute-for-religious-freedom.

6. Timothy O'Neill, "Zorach v. Clauson (1952)," *First Amendment Encyclopedia*, 2009, accessed June 7, 2022, https://www.mtsu.edu/first-amendment/article/677/zorach-v-clauson.

CHAPTER 6

1. J. A. Swezey and K. G. Schultz, "Released-Time Programs in Religion Education," Faculty Publications and Presentations, Paper 226, (2013), accessed March 23, 2022, http://digitalcommons.liberty.edu/educ_fac_pubs/226. Reprinted from *Religion in the Public School: Negotiating the New Commons*, ed. M. D. Waggoner (Lanham, MD: Rowman and Littlefield, 2013), 6.

2. "History," *ReleasedTime.org*, 1999, accessed May 22, 2022, https://releasedtime.org/history.

3. Swezey. 4.

4. Swezey, 6.

5. "Legality," *ReleasedTime.org*, 1999. accessed May 22, 2022, https://releasedtime.org/legality.

6. Swezey, 7.

7 "History," *ReleasedTime.org*, 1999, accessed May 22, 2022, https://releasedtime.org/history.

8. M. Riser-Kositsky, "Education Statistics: Facts About American Schools," *Education Week*, January 3, 2019, https://www.edweek.org/leadership/education-statistics-facts-about-american-schools/2019/01.

CHAPTER 7

1. "I Have Gotten a Lot of Results! I Know Several Thousand Things That Won't Work," Quote Investigator, July 31, 2012, https://quoteinvestigator.com/2012/07/31/edison-lot-results/.

2. Thermal exhaust port. I'm sure you all knew that off the top of your head, just like I did, right?

CHAPTER 9

1. "Art Movement Definition," Eden Gallery Art Blog, September 24, 2021, accessed September 27, 2022, https://www.eden-gallery.com/news/art-movement-definition.

2. The Peter Kreeft quotation is well-known, but its original source or book is unclear.

APPENDIX 2

1. Spallino, "How Character Education Helps Children Learn and Develop."

2. Peter C. Hill and Kenneth I. Pargament, "Advances in the Conceptualization and Measurement of Religion and Spirituality: Implications for Physical and Mental Health Research," *American Psychologist* 58, no. 1 (2003), 68, DOI: 10.1037/0003-066X.58.1.64.

3. Morris, 3.

4. Stark, 53.

5. Dein, 5 emphasis added.

6. Samuel R. Weber and Kenneth I. Pargament, "The Role of Religion and Spirituality in Mental Health," *Current Opinion in Psychiatry* 27, no. 5 (2014), 359.

7. Harold G. Koenig, "Religion and Medicine II: Religion, Mental Health, and Related Behaviors." *The International Journal of Psychiatry in Medicine* 31, no. 1 (2001), 102.

8. Koenig, 103.

9. Y. Joel Wong, Lynn Rew, and Kristina D. Slaikeu, "A Systematic Review of Recent Research on Adolescent Relgiosity/Spirituality and Mental Health," *Issues in Mental Health Nursing* 27 (2006): 162, https://www.researchgate.net/profile/Y-Joel-Wong/publication/7354505_A_systematic_review_of_recent_research_on_adolescent_religiosityspirituality_and_mental_health/links/54bd4b680cf27c8f2814b51a/A-systematic-review-of-recent-research-on-adolescent-religiosity-spirituality-and-mental-health.pdf.

10. "Youth Risk Behavior Survey: Data Summary & Trends Report 2009–2019," CDC, 2019, www.cdc.gov/healthyyouth.

11. Stark, 86.

12. Ibid.

13. Stark, 81–82.

14. Maria Archer, "The Positive Effects of Religion on Mental Illness."

15. Weber and Pargament, 358.

16. Koenig and Larson, 71.

17. Ibid, 72.

18. Koenig, 99.

19. Rachael Rettner, "God Help Us? How Religion is Good (and Bad) for Mental Health," LIVEScience, September 23, 2015, https://www.livescience.com/52197-religion-mental-health-brain.html.

20. Scott Schieman, Alex Bierman, and Christopher G. Ellison, "Religion and Mental Health," In *Handbook of the Sociology of Mental Health* (Springer, Dordrecht, 2013), 467.

21. Rettner, "God Help Us?"

22. Weber and Pargament, 359.

23. Sian Cotton, Kathy Zebracki, Susan L. Rosenthal, Joel Tsevat, and Dennis Drotar, "Religion/Spirituality and Adolescent Health Outcomes: A Review," *Journal of Adolescent Health* 38, no. 4 (2006), 472.

24. Stark, 105.

25. Cotton, Zebracki, Rosenthal, Tsevat, et al, 476.

26. Maria Archer, "The Positive Effects of Religion on Mental Illness."

27. Hill, 67.

28. Koenig and Larson, 71.

29. Stark, 106.

30. Regnerus, "Making the Grade," 5.

31. Stark, 140.

32. Lisa J. Bridges with Kristin A. Moore, "Religion and Spirituality in Childhood and Adolescence," *Child Trends* (January 2002), accessed March 31, 2022, 45, https://eclass.uoa.gr/modules/document/file.php/PPP265/Religion%20and%20Spirituality.pdf.

33. Barrett, 451.

34. Morris, 3.

35. Hodge, 145–46.

36. Regnerus, "Making the Grade," 8.

37. Ibid, 10.

38. Stark, 138–39.

39. Jeynes, "Religiosity, Religious Schools, and Their Relationship with the Achievement Gap," 273.

40. Stark, 48.

BIBLIOGRAPHY

Abdel-Khalek, Ahmed M. "Religiosity, Health and Happiness: Significant Relations in Adolescents from Qatar." *ISJP* 60, no. 7 (2014): 656–661. DOI:10.1177/0020764013511792.

Acar, Erkan. "Effects of Social Capital on Academic Success: A Narrative Synthesis." *Educational Research and Reviews* 6, no. 6 (June 2011): 456–461. Accessed May 26, 2022. http://www.academicjournals.org/ERR.

"ACT Test Scores in US Fall to Lowest in 30 Years." VOA News. October 15, 2022. Accessed December 20, 2022. https://learningenglish.voanews.com/a/act-test-scores-in-us-fall-to-lowest-in-30-years/6788531.html.

American Board. "11 Facts About the History of Education in America." July 1, 2015. Accessed March 14, 2022. https://www.americanboard.org/blog/11-facts-about-the-history-of-education-in-america/.

Anderson, Meg and Kavitha Cardoza. "Mental Health in Schools: A Hidden Crisis Affecting Millions of Students." nprED. August 31, 2016. https://www.npr.org/sections/ed/2016/08/31/464727159/mental-health-in-schools-a-hidden-crisis-affecting-millions-of-students.

Archer, Maria. The Positive Effects of Religion on Mental Illness. Institute for Family Studies. July 28, 2017. https://ifstudies.org/blog/the-positive-effects-of-religion-on-mental-illness.

Arnold, Matthieu. "Martin Luther and Education." *Lutheran Quarterly* 33 (2019): 287-303.

"Art Movement Definition." Eden Gallery Art Blog. September 24, 2021. Accessed September 27, 2022. https://www.eden-gallery.com/news/art-movement-definition

"ASCD Whole Child Network." *HundrED.org*. Accessed March 15, 2022. https://hundred.org/en/innovations/ascd-whole-child-network#054768af.

Baier, Dirk. "The Influence of Religiosity on Violent Behavior of Adolescents: A Comparison of Christian and Muslim Religiosity." *Journal of Interpersonal Violence* 29, no. 1 (2014): 102–127. DOI: 10.1177/0886260513504646.

Baker, John S., Jr. "Wall of Separation." *First Amendment Encyclopedia*. 2009. Accessed June 7, 2022. https://www.mtsu.edu/first-amendment/article/886/wall-of-separation.

Barnwell, Paul. "Students' Broken Moral Compasses." *The Atlantic*. July 25, 2016. Accessed December 30, 2022. https://www.theatlantic.com/education/archive/2016/07/students-broken-moral-compasses/492866/.

Barrett, Brian. "Religion and Habitus: Exploring the Relationship between Religious Involvement and Educational Outcomes and Orientations among Urban African American Students." *Urban Education* 45, no. 4 (2010): 448-479. Accessed March 22, 2022. DOI: 10.1177/0042085910372349.

Barry, John M. "God, Government, and Roger Williams' Big Idea." *Smithsonian Magazine*. January 2012. Accessed June 7, 2022. https://www.smithsonianmag.com/history/god-government-and-roger-williams-big-idea-6291280/.

Barshay, Jill. "Proof Points: Why Reading Comprehension Is Deteriorating." The Hechinger Report. May 17, 2021. Accessed December 20, 2022. https://hechingerreport.org/proof-points-why-reading-comprehension-is-deteriorating/.

Bartkowski, John P., Xiaohe Xu, and Stephen Bartkowski. "Mixed Blessing: The Beneficial and Detrimental Effects of Religion on Child Development Among Third-Graders." *Religions* 10, no. 37 (2019): 1–18. doi:10.3390/rel10010037.

Benson, Clarence H. *A Popular History of Christian Education*. Chicago: Moody Press, 1943.

Bergin, Christi and Sara Prewett. "The Pros of Prosocial." September 1, 2020. Accessed May 18, 2022. https://www.naesp.org/resource/the-pros-of-prosocial/.

Berthold, Anne, and Willibald Ruch. "Satisfaction with Life and Character Strengths of Non-Religious and Religious People: It's Practicing One's Religion That Makes the Difference." *Frontiers in Psychology* 5, no. 876 (August 2014). https://doi.org/10.3389/fpsyg.2014.00876.

"The Bible and the Common Schools." *The Biblical World* 20, no. 4 (1902): 243–247. https://www.jstor.org/stable/3137394.

Biden, Joe. "Remarks by President Biden at the 2022 National and State Teachers of the Year Event." April 27, 2022. Accessed April 8, 2022. https://www.whitehouse.gov/briefing-room/speeches-remarks/2022/04/27/remarks-by-president-biden-at-the-2022-national-and-state-teachers-of-the-year-event/.

"BLS History." Boston Latin School. Accessed April 22, 2022. https://www.bls.org/apps/pages/index.jsp?uREC_ID=206116&type=d.

Bolden, Felicia. "Narrowing Achievement Gaps for At-Risk Students." Educator's Blog. February 13, 2020. Accessed December 20, 2022. https://www.graduateprogram.org/2020/02/narrowing-achievement-gaps-for-at-risk-students/.

Boppart, Timo, Josef Falkinger, and Volker Grossmann. "Protestantism and Education: Reading (the Bible) and Other Skills." Beiträge zur Jahrestagung des Vereins für Socialpolitik 2011: Die Ordnung der Weltwirtschaft: Lektionen aus der Krise- Session: Economics of Religion, No. D8-V2 (2011). http://hdl.handle.net/10419/48732.

Bowers, Hannah S. "John Calvin's Philosophy of Education." Blog post. September 30, 2013. Accessed May 15, 2022. https://coffeeshopthinking.wordpress.com/2013/09/30/john-calvins-philosophy-of-education/.

Bowers, Hannah S. "John Dewey's Philosophy of Education." Blog Post. September 23, 2013. Accessed November 1, 2022. https://coffeeshopthinking.wordpress.com/2013/09/23/john-deweys-philosophy-of-education/.

Braam, Arjan W. and Harold G. Koenig. "Religion, Spirituality, and Depression in Prospective Studies: A Systematic Review." *Journal of Affective Disorders* 257 (2019): 428–438. https://doi.org/10.1016/j.jad.2019.06.063.

Brangham, William, and Gretchen Frazee. "Growing Number of Young Americans Feel Climate Anxiety." PBS NewsHour. November 10, 2021. Accessed December 20, 2022. https://www.pbs.org/newshour/show/growing-number-of-young-americans-feel-climate-anxiety-heres-what-they-need-to-cope.

Bridges, Lisa J. with Kristin A. Moore. "Religion and Spirituality in Childhood and Adolescence." *Child Trends* (January 2002). Accessed March 31, 2022. https://eclass.uoa.gr/modules/document/file.php/PPP265/Religion%20and%20Spirituality.pdf.

Brown, Nathan, Bill Kissane, and John Madeley. "Constitutionalism, Religion and Education." *American Behavioral Scientist* 60, no. 8 (2016): 1013-1035.

"Bullying and Cyberbullying." SchoolSafety.gov. 2022. Accessed December 20, 2022. https://www.schoolsafety.gov/bullying-and-cyberbullying?subtopic%5B107%5D=107#-block-views-block-resources-by-subtopic-block-1.

Carleton, David. "Horace Mann." *The First Amendment Encyclopedia*. 2009. Accessed November 30, 2022. https://mtsu.edu/first-amendment/article/1283/horace-mann.

Carleton, David. "Old Deluder Satan Act of 1647." *First Amendment Encyclopedia*. 2009. Accessed November 11, 2022. https://www.mtsu.edu/first-amendment/article/1032/old-deluder-satan-act-of-1647.

Carr, Peggy G. "Commissioner's Statement on the Upcoming Release of NAEP Long-Term Trend Assessment Results." August 31, 2022. Accessed September 1, 2022. https://nces.ed.gov/whatsnew/commissioner/remarks2022/8_31_2022.asp.

Chancey, Mark A. "Bible Bills, Bible Curricula, and Controversies of Biblical Proportions: Legislative Efforts to Promote Bible Courses in Public Schools." *Religion and Education* 34:, no. 1 (2007): 28–47. Accessed March 22, 2022. DOI: 10.1080/15507394.2007.10012390.

Chancey, Mark. "Public School Bible Courses in Historical Perspective: North Carolina as a Case Study." Religion & Education 40, no. 3 (2013): 253–269. DOI:10.1080/15507394.2013.804356.

Chen, Grace. "A Relevant History of Public Education in the United States." *Public School Review*. February 17, 2021. Accessed March 14, 2022. https://www.publicschoolreview.com/blog/a-relevant-history-of-public-education-in-the-united-states.

"Christian Parents Want Education Quality and Their Values Too, According to New Stride, Inc. Survey." Business Wire. August 3, 2022. Accessed October 17, 2022. https://www.businesswire.com/news/home/20220803005183/en/Christian-Parents-Want-Education-Quality-and-Their-Values-Too-According-to-New-Stride-Inc.-Survey.

Clark, Mark. "Is Religious Faith Really Good for Us?" *Outreach Magazine* June 17, 2021. Accessed March 22, 2022. https://outreachmagazine.com/features/discipleship/67339-is-religious-faith-really-good-for-us.html.

Codling, Jim Llewellyn. "John Calvin: An Educational Innovator or a Reflector of Society." *Theses and Dissertations* 2889 (2008). https://scholarsjunction.msstate.edu/td/2889

Colson, Charles. "Reversing Biblical Memory Loss." *Christianity Today* August 5, 2001. Accessed March 22, 2022. https://www.christiainitytoday.com/ct/2001/august6/31.88.html.

"Common School Movement." Education Encyclopedia. 2022. Accessed November 20, 2022. https://education.stateuniversity.com/pages/1871/Common-School-Movement.html.

Conroy, J.C. "Does Religious Education Work? A Three-Year Investigation into the Practices and Outcomes of Religious Education: A Briefing Paper." University of Glasgow (2011). Accessed March 22, 2022. https://www.secularism.org.uk/uploads/does-religious-education-work-by-prof-c-conroy.pdf.

Cotton, Sian, Kathy Zebracki, Susan L. Rosenthal, Joel Tsevat, and Dennis Drotar. "Religion/Spirituality and Adolescent Health Outcomes: A Review." *Journal of Adolescent Health* 38, no. 4 (2006): 472–480.

Culture Translator. "Mr. Beast's Burgers, Rings of Sour, and Spoonies." Axis.org email. https://app.axis.org/explore/ctp-2022-09-09.

"Data and Statistics on Children's Mental Health." CDC. June 3, 2022. Accessed December 20, 2022. https://www.cdc.gov/childrensmentalhealth/data.html.

Dein, Simon, Christopher CH Cook, and Harold Koenig. "Religion, Spirituality, and Mental Health: Current Controversies and Future Directions." *The Journal of Nervous and Mental Disease* 200, no. 10 (2012): 852–855.

Desilver, Drew. "U.S. Students' Academic Achievement Still Lags That of Their Peers in Many Other Countries." Pew Research Center. February 15, 2017. Accessed December 20, 2022. https://www.pewresearch.org/fact-tank/2017/02/15/u-s-students-internationally-math-science/.

"Effects of Religious Practice on Education." Marripedia. Accessed June 9, 2022. https://marripedia.org/effects_of_religious_practice_on_education.

Ellison, Christopher G. and Jeffery S. Levin. "The Religion-Health Connection: Evidence, Theory, and Future Directions." *Health Education & Behavior* 25, no. 6 (December 1998): 700–720. Accessed March 31, 2022. https://csrs.nd.edu/assets/59929/ellison_and_levin_1998.pdf.

Ericsson, Samuel E., Kimberlee Colby, Robert Payne, and Stephen Crawford. *Religious Released Time Education: The Overlooked Open Door in Public Schools.* ERIC Clearinghouse, 1982.

Estrada, Crystal Amiel M., Marian Fe Theresa C. Lomboy, Ernesto R. Gregorio Jr., Emmy Amalia, Cynthia R. Leynes, Romeo R. Quizon, and Jun Kobayashi. "Religious Education Can Contribute to Adolescent Mental Health in School Settings." *International Journal of Mental Health Systems* 13, no. 28 (2019): 1–6. https://doi.org/10.1186/s13033-019-0286-7.

"Facts About Bullying." StopBullying.gov. September 9, 2021. Accessed December 20, 2022. https://www.stopbullying.gov/resources/facts.

Fagan, Patrick F. "Religious Practice and Educational Attainment." *MarriResearch* (2010). https://downloads.frc.org/EF/EF12D59.pdf.

"Fast Facts: Bullying." NCES. 2022. Accessed December 20, 2022. https://nces.ed.gov/fastfacts/display.asp?id=719.

"Fast Facts: Long-term Trends in Reading and Mathematics Achievement." NCES. 2022. Accessed December 20, 2022. https://nces.ed.gov/fastfacts/display.asp?id=38.

"Fast Facts: Mathematics." NCES. 2022. Accessed December 20, 2022. https://nces.ed.gov/fastfacts/display.asp?id=514.

"Fast Facts: Reading." NCES. 2022. Accessed December 20, 2022. https://nces.ed.gov/fastfacts/display.asp?id=147.

"Fast Facts: School Crime." NCES. 2022. Accessed December 20, 2022. https://nces.ed.gov/fastfacts/display.asp?id=49.

Feldman, Derrick. "Social Movements for Good: What They Are and How to Lead Them." Philanthropy-Impact.org. Accessed September 27, 2022. https://www.philanthropy-impact.

org/expert-opinion/social-movements-good-what-they-are-and-how-lead-them.

Foley, Ryan. "63% of Americans Think Parents Should Have 'Final Say' in Education." *The Christian Post*. November 20, 2021. Accessed October 18, 2022. https://www.christianpost.com/news/parents-should-have-final-say-in-public-education-survey.html.

"For the Skeptic." Released Time Education. Accessed March 23, 2022. https://www.rtce.org/skeptics.html.

Freedom Forum Institute. "The First Amendment Says Nothing About 'Separation of Church and State.'" *Freedom Forum Institute*. 2022. Accessed June 7, 2022. https://www.freedomforuminstitute.org/about/faq/the-first-amendment-says-nothing-about-separation-of-church-and-state-or-a-wall-of-separation-between-church-and-state-where-did-this-idea-come-from-is-it-really/.

Fukofuka, Sunia. "The Impact of Spirituality on Academic Performance." *International Forum*. 10, no. 2 (October 2007): 35-48. Accessed May 21, 2022. https://scholar.google.com.ph/citations?view_op=view_citation&hl=en&user=0Os8InUAAAAJ&citation_for_view=0Os8InUAAAAJ:u5HHmVD_uO8C.

Gamble, Richard M., ed. *The Great Tradition: Classic Readings on What It Means to Be an Educated Human Being*. Wilmington, DE: ISI Press, 2009.

Garris, Zachary. "The Secularization of American Public Schools." Teach Diligently. September 14, 2015. Accessed November 30, 2022. https://teachdiligently.com/articles/the-secularization-of-american-public-schools.

Glaskin, Max. "The Science Behind Spokes." Cyclist UK. April 28, 2015. Accessed October 13, 2022. https://www.cyclist.co.uk/in-depth/85/the-science-behind-spokes.

Goncalves, Juliane Piasseschi de Bernardin, Clarice Sandi Madruga, Giancarlo Lucchetti, Maria do Rosário Dias Latorre, Ronaldo Laranjeira, and Homero Vallada. "The Effect of Religiosity on Violence: Results from a Brazilian Population-Based Representative Sample of 4,607 Individuals." *Plos One* 15, no. 8 (2020): 1–14. https://doi.org/10.1371/journal.pone.0238020.

Grady, Sarah, "A Fresh Look at Homeschooling in the U.S." NCES Blog. Sept. 26, 2017. Accessed July 10, 2020. https://nces.ed.gov/blogs/nces/post/a-fresh-look-at-homeschooling-in-the-u-s.

Hall, D. *The Legacy of John Calvin: His Influence on the Modern World*. Phillipsburg, NJ: P & R Publishing, 2008.

Hallett, Michael, and Byron R. Johnson. "The New Prison Ministry Lies in Bible Education." *Christianity Today*. October 19, 2021. Accessed March 22, 2022. https://www.christianitytoday.com/ct/2021/november/christian-prison-ministry-bible-education-seminary.html.

Harris, Matthew. "Virginia Statute for Religious Freedom." *First Amendment Encyclopedia*. 2009. Accessed June 7, 2022. https://mtsu.edu/first-amendment/article/880/virginia-statute-for-religious-freedom.

Hildebrand, David. "John Dewey." *The Stanford Encyclopedia of Philosophy*. Edward N. Zalta, ed. Winter 2021. Accessed May 11, 2022. https://plato.stanford.edu/archives/win2021/entries/dewey/.

Hill, Brian V. "Values in Free Fall? Religious Education and Values in Public Schools." *Journal of Christian Education* 51, no. 3 (2008): 43–55.

Hill, Peter C., and Kenneth I. Pargament. "Advances in the Conceptualization and Measurement of Religion and Spirituality: Implications for Physical and Mental Health Research." *American Psychologist* 58, no. 1 (2003): 64–74. DOI: 10.1037/0003-066X.58.1.64.

"History of RTCE." Released Time Education. Accessed March 23, 2022. www.rtce.org/history.

Hodge, David R. "Latino Students and Spiritual Release Time Programs: Does Releasing Students from Class for Spiritual Instruction Impede Academic Achievement?" *Families in Society: The Journal of Contemporary Social Services* 93, no. 2 (2012): 141–150.

Hodge, David R., and Gary S. Cuddeback. "Release Time and Academic Outcomes: Does Releasing Students for Religious or Moral Education. Negatively Affect Test Scores?" *Journal of the Society for Social Work and Research* 1, no. 1 (2010): 56–65. Accessed May 19, 2020. doi:10.5243/jsswr.2010.5.

Horwitz, Ilana M., Benjamin W. Domingue, and Kathleen Mullan Harris. "Not a Family Matter: The Effects of Religiosity on Academic Outcomes Based on Evidence from Siblings." *Social Science Research* (2020): 88–89. Accessed May 27, 2022. https://doi.org/10.1016/j.ssresearch.2020.102426.

"How Students Can Benefit from Character Education." Teachnology.com. Accessed May 26, 2022. https://www.teach-nology.com/currenttrends/character_education/.

Howerton, Josh. "No, Christianity Is Not as Bad as You Think: 5 Statistics That Reveal It's Good for the World." *The Gospel Coalition*. March 19, 2022. Accessed March 22, 2022. https://www.thegospelcoalition.org/article/christianity-not-bad/.

Hudson, David L., Jr. "Engel v. Vitale (1962)." *First Amendment Encyclopedia*. 2009. Accessed June 7, 2022. https://www.mtsu.edu/first-amendment/article/665/engel-v-vitale.

"I Have Gotten a Lot of Results! I Know Several Thousand Things That Won't Work." Quote Investigator. July 31, 2012. https://quoteinvestigator.com/2012/07/31/edison-lot-results/.

Jensen, Larry and Holly Passey. "Moral Education Curricula in the Public Schools." *Religion and Public Education* 20 (1–3): 27–35. DOI: 10.1080/10567224.1993.11000764.

Jeynes, William H. "The Effects of Religious Commitment on the Academic Achievement of Black and Hispanic Children." *Urban Education* 34, no. 4 (1999): 458–479. http://citeseerx.ist.psu.edu/viewdoc/download?doi=10.1.1.860.6145&rep=rep1&type=pdf.

Jeynes, William H. "A Meta-Analysis of the Efficacy of Different Types of Parental Involvement Programs for Urban Students." *Urban Education* 47, no. 4 (2012): 706–742. Accessed March 22, 2022. DOI: 10.1177/0042085912445643.

Jeynes, William H. "A Meta-Analysis on the Relationship Between Prayer and Student Outcomes." *Education and Urban Society* 52, no. 8 (2020): 1223–1237.

Jeynes, William H. "The Relationship Between Bible Literacy and Behavioral and Academic Outcomes in Urban Areas: A Meta-Analysis." *Education and Urban Society* 42, no. 5 (2010): 522–544.

Jeynes, William H. "Religiosity, Religious Schools, and Their Relationship with the Achievement Gap: A Research Synthesis and Meta-Analysis." *The Journal of Negro Education* 79, no. 3 (2010): 263–79. Accessed May 14, 2020. www.jstor.org/stable/20798348.

Kahn, N.F. and R. Graham, eds. "The Current Landscape of Adolescent Risk Behavior." In *Promoting Positive Adolescent Health Behaviors and Outcomes: Thriving in the 21st Century*. Washington, DC: National Academies Press, 2019. https://www.ncbi.nlm.nih.gov/books/NBK554988/

Katz, Michael B. "The Origins of Public Education: A Reassessment." *History of Education Quarterly* 16, no. 4 (Winter 1976): 381–407. http://www.jstor.org/stable/367722.

Keller-Cohen, Deborah. "Rethinking Literacy: Comparing Colonial and Contemporary America." *Anthropology & Education Quarterly* 24, no. 4 (December 1993): 288–307. Accessed November 23, 2022. https://www.jstor.org/stable/3195932.

King, Barbara. "A Study of Religious Education: Its Nature, Its Aims, Its Manifestations." *Honors*

Projects 31 (1960). https://digitalcommons.iwu.edu/socanth_honproj/31.

King, Pamela Ebstyne, and James L. Furrow. "Religion as a Resource for Positive Youth Development: Religion, Social Capital, and Moral Outcomes." *Developmental Psychology* 40, no. 5 (2004): 703–713. DOI: 10.1037/0012-1649.40.5.703.

Koenig, Harold G. "Religion and Medicine II: Religion, Mental Health, and Related Behaviors." *The International Journal of Psychiatry in Medicine* 31, no. 1 (2001): 97–109.

Koenig, Harold G., and David B. Larson. "Religion and mental health: Evidence for an association." *International Review of Psychiatry* 13, no. 2 (2001): 67–78.

Lara, Julia and Kenneth Noble. "Chronic Absenteeism." NEA Research Brief 57 (2018). Accessed November 2, 2022. https://files.eric.ed.gov/fulltext/ED595241.pdf.

"Legality." ReleasedTime.org. 1999. Accessed May 22, 2022. https://releasedtime.org/legality.

Levin, Jeff. "Religion and Mental Health: Theory and Research." *International Journal of Applied Psychoanalytic Studies*. (2010). Accessed March 31, 2022. DOI: 10.1002/aps.240.

Levin, Jeffery S., Linda M. Chatters, and Robert Joseph Taylor. "Religious Effects on Health Status and Life Satisfaction Among Black Americans." *Journal of Gerontology* 50B, no. 3 (1995): S154–S163.

Levin, Jeffery S., Kyriakos S. Markides, and Laura A. Ray. "Religious Attendance and Psychological Well-Being in Mexican Americans: A Panel Analysis of Three-Generations Data." *The Gerontologist* 36, no. 4 (1996): 454-463. https://academic.oup.com/gerontologist/article/36/4/454/612370.

Lewis, C. S. *Mere Christianity*. New York: Book-of-the-Month Club, 1997.

Lickona, Thomas. "Character Education: The Heart of School Reform." *Religion & Education* 27, no. 1 (2000): 58–64. https://doi.org/10.1080/15507394.2000.11000917.

Lippy, Charles H. "Christian Nation or Pluralistic Culture: Religion in American Life." In *Multicultural Education: Issues and Perspectives*, 9th ed., edited by James A Banks and Cherry A. McGee Banks, 59–78. Hoboken, NJ: Wiley & Sons, 2016.

Logan, Jessica, et. al. "Has Ohio's Third-Grade Reading Guarantee Led to Reading Improvements?" The Ohio State University CCEC. Spring 2019. Accessed December 20, 2022. https://crane.osu.edu/files/2020/01/Third-Grade-Reading-Whitepaper_032019_WEB2-1.pdf.

Lynn, Barry. "Bible Curriculum and Public Schools: Oil and Water." *Religion & Education* 27, no. 1 (2000): 28–33. Accessed March 22, 2022. DOI: 10.1080/15507394.2000.11000912

Madigan, Jennifer C. "The Education of Women and Girls in the United States: A Historical Perspective." *Advances in Gender and Education* (2009): 11–13. https://scholarworks.sjsu.edu/second_ed_pub.

Margalit, Liraz. "The Psychology of Choice." *Psychology Today* October 3, 2014. Accessed November 20, 2022. https://www.psychologytoday.com/us/blog/behind-online-behavior/201410/the-psychology-choice.

Marquand, Robert. "The Rise and Fall of the Bible in US Classrooms." *The Christian Science Monitor* September 5, 1985. Accessed April 24, 2022. https://www.csmonitor.com/1985/0905/dback3-f.html#.

Masci, David. "Darwin and His Theory of Evolution." February 4, 2009. Accessed May 11, 2022. https://www.pewresearch.org/religion/2009/02/04/darwin-and-his-theory-of-evolution/.

McCollister, Betty. "Religion and Schools: The Problem of Released Time." *Religion & Public*

Education 12, no. 1–2 (1985): 14–16. DOI: 10.1080/10567224.1985.11487840.

"Mental Health." CDC. September 12, 2022. Accessed December 20, 2022. https://www.cdc.gov/healthyyouth/mental-health/index.htm.

Mitropoulos, Arielle. "Thousands of Students Reported 'Missing' from School Systems Nationwide Amid Covid-19 Pandemic." ABC News. March 2, 2021. Accessed October 18, 2022. https://abcnews.go.com/US/thousands-students-reported-missing-school-systems-nationwide-amid/story?id=76063922.

Monaghan, E. Jennifer. "Literacy Instruction and Gender in Colonial New England." *American Quarterly* 40, no. 1 (March 1988): 18–41. Accessed November 23, 2022. https://www.jstor.org/stable/2713140.

Morris, Monique W., Barry Krisberg, and Sharan Dhanoa. "Summary of Findings: Released Time Bible Education." (2003) National Council on Crime and Delinquency. Accessed May 2020. https://california.foundationcenter.org/reports/summary-of-findings-released-time-bible-education/.

Myers, Jeff. *Truth Changes Everything.* Grand Rapids: Baker Books, 2022.

Myers, Jeff. *Unquestioned Answers: Rethinking Ten Christian Cliches to Rediscover Biblical Truths.* Colorado Springs, CO: David C Cook, 2020.

"NAEP Long-Term Trend Assessment Results: Reading and Mathematics." NAEP. 2022. Accessed December 20, 2022. https://www.nationsreportcard.gov/ltt/?age=9.

"NAEP Report Card: 2019 NAEP Reading Assessment." NAEP. 2019. Accessed December 20, 2022. https://www.nationsreportcard.gov/highlights/reading/2019/g12/.

"NAEP Report Card: 2019 NAEP Mathematics Assessment." NAEP. 2019. Accessed December 20, 2022. https://www.nationsreportcard.gov/highlights/mathematics/2019/g12/.

"NAEP Report Card: 2022 NAEP Reading Assessment." NAEP. 2022. Accessed December 20, 2022. https://www.nationsreportcard.gov/highlights/reading/2022/.

"NAEP Report Card: 2022 NAEP Mathematics Assessment." NAEP. 2022. Accessed December 20, 2022. https://www.nationsreportcard.gov/highlights/mathematics/2022/.

Naylor, Natalie. "The Bible in American Education: From Source Book to Textbook." David L. Barr and Nicholas Piediscalzi, eds. *National Council on Religion and Public Education* 10, no. 2 (1983): 20–21. DOI: 10.1080/15507386.1983.11487712.

Nieuwhof, Carey. "Think Again: Why Religion is Good for Us." Accessed August 2, 2022. https://careynieuwhof.com/think-again-why-religion-is-good-for-us/.

Novis-Deutsch, Nurit, Haym Dayan, Yehuda Pollak, and Mona Khoury-Kassabri. "Religiosity as a Moderator of ADHD-Related Antisocial Behavior and Emotional Distress Among Secular, Religious, and Ultra-Orthodox Jews in Israel." *IJSP* (2021): 1–10. DOI: 10.1177/00207640211005501.

Ohio Education By The Numbers 2022. Thomas Fordham Institute. 2022. Accessed April 20, 2022. https://www.ohiobythenumbers.com.

"Ohio's Whole Child Framework." Ohio Department of Education. June 27, 2022. Accessed August 31, 2022. https://education.ohio.gov/Topics/Student-Supports/Ohios-Whole-Child-Framework.

O'Neill, Timothy. "Zorach v. Clauson (1952)." *First Amendment Encyclopedia.* 2009. Accessed June 7, 2022. https://www.mtsu.edu/first-amendment/article/677/zorach-v-clauson.

"Parent, Family, Community Involvement in Education." NEA Policy Brief. 2008. https://www.

coursehero.com/file/35617307/NEA-Poliy-Brief-Parent-Family-Community-Involvmentpdf/.

Pattaro, Chiara. "Character Education: Themes and Researches. An Academic Literature Review." *Italian Journal of Sociology of Education* 8, no. 1 (2016). DOI: 10.14658/pupj-ijse-2016-1-2.

Piedra, Alberto M. "The Tragedy of American Education: The Role of John Dewey." The Institute of World Politics. February 1, 2018. Accessed May 11, 2022. https://www.iwp.edu/articles/2018/02/01/the-tragedy-of-american-education-the-role-of-john-dewey/.

"Private School FAQs." Council for American Private Education. 2020. Accessed July 10, 2020. https://www.capenet.org/facts.html.

Rafi, Mahdi Abdollahzadeh, Maryam Hasanzadeh Avval, Abas Ali Yazdani, and Fazel Bahrami. "The Influence of Religiosity on the Emotional-Behavioral Health of Adolescents." *Journal of Religion and Health* 59 (2020): 1870-1888. https://doi.org/10.1007/s10943-018-00747-w.

Regnerus, Mark. D. "Making the Grade: The Influence of Religion upon the Academic Performance of Youth in Disadvantaged Communities." Baylor ISR: Baylor University, 2008. Accessed May 21, 2022. http://www.baylorisr.org/wp-content/uploads/ISR_Making_Grade.pdf.

Regnerus, Mark, Christian Smith, and Melissa Fritsch. "Religion in the Lives of American Adolescents: A Review of the Literature." *A Research Report of the National Study of Youth and Religion* No. 3. Chapel Hill, NC: UNC, 2003. Accessed May 21, 2022. https://files.eric.ed.gov/fulltext/ED473896.pdf.

"Release Time Programs." ADL. March 4, 2017. Accessed March 23, 2022. https://www.adl.org/resources/tools-and-strategies/release-time-programs.

"Released Time Bible Education." *ReleasedTime.org*. 1999. Accessed May 22, 2022. https://releasedtime.org.

Rettner, Rachael. God Help Us? How Religion is Good (and Bad) for Mental Health. LIVEScience. September 23, 2015. https://www.livescience.com/52197-religion-mental-health-brain.html.

Riser-Kositsky, M. "Education Statistics: Facts About American Schools." *Education Week*. January 3, 2019. .https://www.edweek.org/leadership/education-statistics-facts-about-american-schools/2019/01.

Ryman, Hana M., and J. Mark Alcorn. "Establishment Clause (Separation of Church and State)." *First Amendment Encyclopedia*. 2009. Accessed June 7, 2022. https://www.mtsu.edu/first-amendment/article/885/establishment-clause-separation-of-church-and-state.

Schieman, Scott, Alex Bierman, and Christopher G. Ellison. "Religion and Mental Health." In *Handbook of the Sociology of Mental Health*, pp. 457–478. Springer, Dordrecht, 2013.

Schwalbach, Jude. "Combating Value-Neutrality and Creating Classrooms of Character." *The Heritage Foundation*. December 13, 2019. Accessed December 30, 2022. https://www.heritage.org/education/commentary/combating-value-neutrality-and-creating-classrooms-character.

Sheldon, Steven B., and Joyce L. Epstein. "Getting Students to School: Using Family and Community Involvement to Reduce Chronic Absenteeism." *School Community Journal* 14, no. 2 (2004): 39–56. Accessed May 31, 2022. https://files.eric.ed.gov/fulltext/EJ794822.pdf.

Sheldon, Steven B., and Joyce L. Epstein. "Improving Student Behavior and School Discipline with Family and Community Involvement." *Education and Urban Society* 35, no. 1 (2002): 4–26. Accessed May 31, 2022. http://eus.sagepub.com/content/35/1/4.

Shen, Jianping, Xuejin Lu, and Joseph Kretovics. "Improving the Education of Students Placed at Risk through School-University Partnerships." *Educational Horizons* 82, no. 3 (2004): 184–193. https://www.jstor.org/stable/42926499.

Skaggs, Gary, and Nancy Bodenhorn. "Relationships Between Implementing Character Education, Student Behavior, and Student Achievement." *Journal of Advanced Academics* 18, no. 1 (2006): 82–114. https://files.eric.ed.gov/fulltext/EJ753972.pdf.

Smith, Christian. "Theorizing Religious Effects Among American Adolescents." *Journal for the Scientific Study of Religion* 42, no. 1 (2003): 17–30. https://csrs.nd.edu/assets/50016/theorizing_religious_effects_among_american_adolescents.pdf.

Spallino, Jessica. "How Character Education Helps Kids Learn and Develop." Method Schools. January 23, 2017. Accessed October 23, 2022. https://www.methodschools.org/blog/how-character-education-helps-kids-learn-and-develop.

Spielberg, Steven, director. *Jurassic Park*. 1993. Universal, 1993. 127 min.

Spurgeon, Charles Haddon. "Spiritual Knowledge and Its Practical Results." *The Spurgeon Library*. 2017. Accessed October 19, 2022. https://www.spurgeon.org/resource-library/sermons/spiritual-knowledge-and-its-practical-results/#flipbook/.

Stark, Rodney. *America's Blessings: How Religion Benefits Everyone, Including Atheists*. Conshohocken, PA: Templeton Press, 2012.

Stephens, Maria, et. al. "Changes between 2011 and 2019 in Achievement Gaps Between High- and Low-Performing Students in Mathematics and Science: International Results From TIMSS." IES. October 2022. Accessed December 20, 2022. https://nces.ed.gov/pubs2022/2022041.pdf.

Steward, Robbie J., and Hanik Jo. "Does Spirituality Influence Academic Achievement and Psychological Adjustment of African American Urban Adolescents? (1998). https://files.eric.ed.gov/fulltext/ED417248.pdf.

Strobel, Lee. *The Case for Faith*. Grand Rapids, MI: Zondervan, 2000.

Swezey, J. A., and K. G. Schultz. "Released-Time Programs in Religion Education." Faculty Publications and Presentations. Paper 226. (2013). Accessed March 23, 2022. http://digitalcommons.liberty.edu/educ_fac_pubs/226. Reprinted from *Religion in the Public School: Negotiating the New Commons*. ed. M. D. Waggoner (Lanham, MD: Rowman and Littlefield, 2013), 77–90.

Thattai, Deeptha V. "A History of Public Education in the United States Editorial Summary." *ResearchGate* (2017). https://www.researchgate.net/publication/321179948.

Toldson, Ivory A., and Kenneth Alonzo Anderson. "Editor's Comment: The Role of Religion in Promoting Academic Success for Black Students." *The Journal of Negro Education* 79, no. 3 (2010): 205–13. Accessed May 19, 2020. www.jstor.org/stable/20798343.

Treleaven, Lisa M. "Quantitative Insights into the Academic Outcomes of Homeschools from the Classic Learning Test." *Home School Researcher* 38, no. 1 (2022): 1–13. Accessed December 20, 2022. https://www.nheri.org/wp-content/uploads/2022/12/HSR381-Treleaven-article-only.pdf.

Van Roekel, Dennis. "Parent, Family, Community Involvement in Education." *NEA Policy Brief*. 2008. Accessed May 31, 2022. https://horseheadsdistrict.com/uploadeddocs/ParentInvolvement.pdf.

Vanderweele, Tyler J., and Brendan Case. "Empty Pews Are an American Public Health Crisis." *Christianity Today*. October 19, 2021. Accessed March 22, 2022. https://www.christianitytoday.com/ct/2021/november/church-empty-pews-are-american-public-health-crisis.html.

Vanneman, Alan, Linda Hamilton, and Janet Baldwin Anderson. "Achievement Gaps: How Black and White Students in Public Schools Perform in Mathematics and Reading on the National Assessment of Educational Progress." U.S. Dept. of Education. July 2009. Accessed December 20, 2022. https://nces.ed.gov/nationsreportcard/pdf/studies/2009455.pdf.

Vile, John R. "Abington School District v. Schempp (1963)." *First Amendment Encyclopedia*. 2009. Accessed June 7, 2022. https://www.mtsu.edu/first-amendment/article/1/abington-school-district-v-schempp.

Vile, John. R. "Board of Education of the City of Cincinnati v. Minor (1872)." *First Amendment Encyclopedia*. 2009. Accessed May 11, 2022. https://www.mtsu.edu/first-amendment/article/660/board-of-education-of-the-city-of-cincinnati-v-minor.

Vile, John R. "Illinois ex rel. McCollum v. Board of Education (1948)." *First Amendment Encyclopedia*. 2009. Accessed June 7, 2022. https://www.mtsu.edu/first-amendment/article/668/illinois-ex-rel-mccollum-v-board-of-education.

Wagner, L. and W. Ruch. "Good Character at School: Positive Classroom Behavior Mediates the Link between Character Strengths and School Achievement." *Frontiers in Psychology* 6, no. 610 (2015). Accessed October 31, 2022. DOI:10.3389/fpsyg.2015.00610.

Ward, Artemus. "Everson v. Board of Education (1947)." *First Amendment Encyclopedia*. 2009. Accessed October 21, 2022. https://mtsu.edu/first-amendment/article/435/everson-v-board-of-education.

Was, Christopher A., Dan J. Woltz, and Clif Drew. "Evaluating Character Education Programs and Missing the Target: A Critique of Existing Research." *Educational Science Review* 1 (2006): 148–156. DOI:10.1016/j.edurev.2006.08.001.

Watson, Stephanie. "How Public Schools Work." HowStuffWorks.com. February 13, 2008. Accessed March 14, 2022. https://people.howstuffworks.com/public-schools.htm.

Weber, Samuel R., and Kenneth I. Pargament. "The Role of Religion and Spirituality in Mental Health." *Current Opinion in Psychiatry* 27, no. 5 (2014): 358–363.

"The Whole Child Approach to Education." ASCD. 2015. Accessed August 31, 2022. http://www.wholechildeducation.org/about/.

Wikipedia. "Abington School District v. Schempp." Last modified October 6, 2022. Accessed October 21, 2022. https://en.wikipedia.org/wiki/Abington_School_District_v._Schempp.

"William Holmes McGuffey and His Readers." *The Museum Gazette*. National Park Service. January 1993. Accessed December 7, 2022. http://www.countryschoolassociation.org/uploads/1/0/0/3/100377070/npsmcguffey__1_.pdf.

"'Wisdom' vs. 'Knowledge': What's the Difference?" Dictionary.com. August 23, 2022. Accessed October 19, 2022. https://www.dictionary.com/e/wisdom-vs-knowledge/.

Wnuk, Marcin. "Links Between Faith and Some Strengths of Character: Religious Commitment Manifestations as Moderators." *Religions* 12 (2021): 786–803. https://doi.org/10.3390/rel12090786.

Woessmann, Ludger, Larissa Zierow, and Benjamin W. Arold. "Religious Education in School Affects Students' Lives in the Long Run." VoxEU. March 3, 2022. Accessed June 9, 2022. https://cepr.org/voxeu/columns/religious-education-school-affects-students-lives-long-run.

Wong, Y. Joel, Lynn Rew, and Kristina D. Slaikeu. "A Systematic Review of Recent Research on Adolescent Relgiosity/Spirituality and Mental Health." *Issues in Mental Health Nursing* 27 (2006): 161–183. https://www.researchgate.net/profile/Y-Joel-Wong/publication/7354505_A_systematic_review_of_recent_research_on_adolescent_religiosityspirituality_and_mental_health/links/54bd4b680cf27c8f2814b51a/A-systematic-review-of-recent-research-on-adolescent-religiosity-spirituality-and-mental-health.pdf.

Wood, J. Luke, and Adriel A. Hilton. "Spirituality and Academic Success: Perceptions of African American Males in the Community College." (2012). https://doi.org/10.1080/15507394.2012.648576.

"Youth Risk Behavior Survey: Data Summary & Trends Report 2009–2019." CDC. 2019. www.cdc.gov/healthyyouth.

Zabilka, Ivan L. "Calvin's Contribution to Universal Education." *The Asbury Theological Journal* **44**, no. 1 (1989): 77–96.

CPSIA information can be obtained
at www.ICGtesting.com
Printed in the USA
LVHW050528030623
748257LV00012B/13